PENHALLOW'S
INDIAN WARS

PENHALLOW'S INDIAN WARS

A Facsimile Reprint
of the
First Edition, Printed in Boston in 1726
With the Notes of Earlier Editors
and Additions from the
Original Manuscript

Notes, Index and Introduction
by
EDWARD WHEELOCK

BOOKS FOR LIBRARIES PRESS
FREEPORT, NEW YORK

First Published 1924
Reprinted 1971

INTERNATIONAL STANDARD BOOK NUMBER:
0-8369-6663-5

LIBRARY OF CONGRESS CATALOG CARD NUMBER:
71-179534

PRINTED IN THE UNITED STATES OF AMERICA
BY
NEW WORLD BOOK MANUFACTURING CO., INC.
HALLANDALE, FLORIDA 33009

Introduction

Penhallow's *History of the Indian Wars* is one of the rarest books of its class. When it first appeared it doubtless was read by some who may have been able to recall the setting up of the first printing press in New England; to most of its early readers the impressions of that first press were familiar objects. Though we may thus associate the book with the earliest of New England imprints, its age alone does not account for the scarcity of surviving copies, for many older books are more common. Its disappearance seems better explained by the fact that matters concerning the Indians were, excepting possibly religious controversies, of the greatest interest to the readers of that time and that such books as these were literally read to pieces; they were issued moreover in only small editions for relatively few readers, as there were probably not 175,000 people in the New England Colonies in 1726.

Here, moreover, the facilities for the preservation of printed matter were in general poor; too often in the outlying settlements the leaky cupboard was the library and the hearth with its flickering pine knot was the study. At the writer's elbow lies a copy of Penhallow's rare *History*, the mutilated survivor of a fireplace accident. The reader of long ago, tiring of the story of the atrocities of the red Indian, or the white man, fell asleep and dropped the book beside him. A live coal now fell upon the little volume and, beginning in the very center of the cover, burned through the first thirty pages, when presumably, the fumes of burning leather awoke J. Hempsted, or the reader of "J. Hempsted, His Book, 1728."

To the New England colonist the depredations of his Indian neighbors were of literally vital interest. The pioneer in the new settlements de-forested his land, tilled his fields, gathered his harvest and, on the Lord's Day, walked to his meeting-house, at all times armed with his flint-lock for self defence against the native whom he had armed at a sinister profit with musket, powder and lead. When at last, Anglo-Saxon determination had conquered and the Indian was eliminated from the problem of pioneer existence, the growing generation of New England boys and girls read into fragments the "Narratives," "Captivities" and "Histories" of those of their forebears who providentially had escaped the enemy, or redeemed after "captivation" had lived to print the tale.

Never before the colonization of America had the English come into continued and intimate contact with savages and in the contest for supremacy that followed, they were but poorly prepared with their incomprehension of primitive society and their ill-conceived policies of fanatical proselytism. On the other hand the Indian of the Altantic coast had experienced little in his acquaintance with the early explorers, English or others, that had prejudiced him favorably toward white men. These had kidnapped him to exhibit him as a curiosity in Europe or to sell him into slavery; they had shot him in little else than wantonness or for petty thievery. When colonization began and the Indian himself had furnished the valuable food-plant without which permanent settlements at that time would probably have failed, he saw his own planting places overrun by cattle, his game driven away, his fisheries ruined by mills and mill-dams, his people destroyed by the firearms, diseases, vices, fire-water, indeed by the very religion of the whites. He was human. Naturally enough, before he was overwhelmed, he devastated outlying settlements and decimated the colonists; during the half century preceding the publication of this *History*, more than eight thousand New England settlers lost their lives and few families there were who mourned no relative or friend. In such a community the interest in Indian affairs was predominant.

A specific instance of this interest is seen in the practice of making Indian affairs the chief topic in the published sermon—the newspaper of that day. Whatever the occasion, this discourse afforded the opportunity for publishing, with appropriate comments, the latest news of important events—conflagrations, marine disasters, earthquakes and the always important accounts of depredations and massacres in the frontier settlements. Our author, for instance, acknowledges his indebtedness for the latest de-

INTRODUCTION.

tails in his narrative of Lovewell's fight (p.115) to such a sermon by the "ingenious Mr. Symmes." He, the minister at Bradford, seems to have secured, by reason of his proximity to the scene of that memorable encounter, "exclusive information" as it would be called in modern journalistic speech and to have hastened its early publication.

Aside from all this, Penhallow's *Indian Wars* seems to have been predestined to become a scarce book. Its author was a public man and perhaps the best known officer of New Hampshire. The various brief biographical sketches of him in books of reference are chiefly abstracts from Nathaniel Adams' Memoir, prefixed to the Reprint of the *Indian Wars* in the *Collections* of the New Hampshire Historical Society, Vol. I, pp. 9-13.

Samuel Penhallow was born in St. Mabon, Cornwall, England, July 2, 1665. In his youth he was a student in the school of the silenced dissenting minister, Charles Morton, at Newington-Green and with Morton, in 1686, he came to New England. It is circumstantially stated that in leaving England, Penhallow had in mind a continuation of his studies under Morton, and, finally, a preparation for missionary labors among the Indians, but his biographer does not seem to have known that his entrance into Harvard College was contemplated. This we learn from a note that some former owner of the Field copy laid into that book. It recites that the Rev. Increase Mather, President of Harvard, received in 1685 a letter from his brother Na-

INTRODUCTION.

thaniel, written "in behalf of this gentleman, ye bearer his kinsman, Mr. Penhallow of Falmouth, in Cornwall, who designs to spend a year or two in New England, in your colledge, for ye prfecting his learning." (Field *Catalogue*, p.255.) With Morton, he remained some time in Charlestown, but we hear no more of his preparation for missionary labors. The political troubles about that time are alleged as the cause of his discouragment.

He next removed to Portsmouth, New Hampshire, where he began a prosperous career in business and political life. Here he married a wealthy heiress, Mary, the daughter of President Cutt, part of whose patrimony was valuable land in Portsmouth. He accumulated what in those times was described as a great estate, but many details of his life have been lost owing in part to the destruction of his diary in the great fire of 1802. He was elected the Speaker of the House, August 7, 1699, and held office for three years. From 1702 to the time of his death, he was an influential member of the Royal Council, holding concurrently the offices of Treasurer of the Province and of Recorder of Deeds. As Councilor, he won popular applause through his controversy with Lieut.-Governor George Vaughan. At that time he was suspended by Vaughan, who was himself soon removed from office by Samuel Shute, the Colonial Governor of Massachusetts and New Hampshire. Penhallow resumed his place and by virtue of his office, took part in the ratification of the treaties with the Indians, of which he has

INTRODUCTION.

given us a description in this history. He was appointed to the Superior Court of Judicature in 1714; of this Court he was Chief-justice when he died December 2, 1726.

He is said to have lived in a style superior to that of most of his fellow townsmen in his brick house at the head of the pier, entertaining every stranger of distinction. His biographer thus describes him as "given to hospitality," wherefore the following Order, found in the *Provincial Papers* of New Hampshire may be of interest, bearing as it does upon the amenities of official life two centuries ago. This directs that:

> "Mr. Treasurer Penhallow take care to provide for the Gentlemen Commrs . . . who are going to Casco fort to the Eastward to publish the Articles of Ratification of peace with the Indians, with all such provisions, wines, Liquors and other necessaries as may be proper . . . " [July 14, 1713.]

Of thirteen children, one son, Captain John Penhallow was an early proprietor of Phipsburg (Georgetown,) Maine, Governor of Arrowsick and a prominent officer of the militia under Col. Thomas Westbrook.

Our author's prominence in official and business life must have stimulated his attention to the Indian affairs of his time and the resulting personal familiarity with his subject is perhaps his strongest claim to authority as a writer of his book. In the publication of this work, he secured a sponsor, if that was needful, in one of the most popular of Boston ministers, Dr. Benjamin Colman, of the Brattle Street Church.

INTRODUCTION.

Dr. Colman looms larger in the enterprise, than at first appears; he ends his Preface after the manner of his profession with the moral that the tale should teach, having begun it by grouping the historians of New England into two classes, "honest and worthy Persons and some learned"—an allusion now obscure, but as he specifically mentions another Indian history, the *Decennium Luctuosum*, by the Rev. Cotton Mather—so often designated as the "learned" Dr. Mather,—we may suspect that he had in mind some attribute of his clerical contemporary. Time may have softened many of the asperities of professional life in the Boston of thirteen thousand inhabitants. Dr. Colman was at the height of his popularity; he had declined the presidency of Harvard College and had published twenty-five of the fifty printed sermons listed by Thomas Prince.

The success of our author's first—and last— literary venture may have been promoted likewise by the reputation of his publishers, Samuel Gerrish and Col. Daniel Henchman, associated in the venture as was common practice of the time. Samuel Gerrish began his business in 1704. He was a member of a prominent family, a son-in-law of Samuel Sewall and a successful publisher. More than fifty books by well-known writers of the day bear his imprint. The last is the *Chronological History* (1736), by Thomas Prince. The first catalogue of books to be sold by auction, so far as known, in this country (1717) was published by him and so likewise the first music-book. Bibliographically his imprints are interesting: "at his Shop in Cornhill," "at the Sign of the Buck over against the South Meeting House" (1711), "lower end of Cornhill," "near the Old Meeting House" (1707), "near the Brick Meeting House," "over against the North side of the Town House in King Street" (1714). In 1712 he was made Fourth Sergeant of the Artillery Company which he had joined in 1709; he was a prominent member of the Old South Church, for several years the Register of Deeds of Suffolk County and for seven years after 1733, the Town Clerk of Boston.

The other publisher, Colonel Daniel Henchman, the most eminent Boston bookseller of his time opened shop, on the south corner of State and Washington Streets, in 1713. To him the Penhallow book must have seemed a small affair indeed, for that year with Benjamin Eliot, he was publishing in folio, the largest book printed till then in Boston. This, *A Compleat Body of Divinity*, by the "Reverend and Learned Samuel Willard," contains more than eleven hundred pages (pagination defective), and its truly imposing list of subscribers accounts for the sale of about seven hundred and fifty copies. It is a nice question whether the size of the edition of such a monumental work may be used as a possible clue to the number of copies of our *Indian Wars* offered for sale the same year. Probably not but we have no other means of knowing. In the case of some other rare little items, variations on the title-page show that reissues were sometimes made to meet unexpected

INTRODUCTION. ix

demands. In this instance the first edition seems to have been the last. Col. Henchman established the first paper mill in New England, in company with his son-in-law Thomas Hancock and others. His property went to Hancock by will and from him, one of the wealthiest men in the Province, a nephew, John Hancock the statesman, inherited a large property.

The name of the printer Thomas Fleet, appears on the title-page in keeping with a custom ending with the century. Originally a London printer, he settled in Boston shortly before 1714, dying in 1758. Many books issued from his press and though "a good man, of great industry, just and benevolent," according to Allen, he was not a good printer, when judged even by the standards of his time. The *Indian Wars* abounds in unskilful and inconsistent typography; misleading errors are plentiful. The much worn type that he used in the book was short of the letter w, yet when he had set out his font, he repeatedly proceeded with a wrong font character, as on page 19, regardless of the appearance of his page.

The book was printed quarto, on a small sheet of English paper. In the middle of each is a fine large heraldic water-mark; careful examination, after unbinding a copy, discloses an escutcheon supported by lions rampant-gardant. Bearing: a pale, charged lozenge. Crest: a large crown. Trimmed to a narrow margin, the book measures about six and seven-sixteenths by four and one-eighth, though the dimension of one copy (Brinley *Catalogue*, No. 415) is given as nearly one-half inch taller. It is bound in sheep, sometimes mistaken for calf, over thin boards. It is finished in carelessly executed blind tooling with two filets about the edges and the back divided into four panels in the same way. It bore no label; the sheets were fastened by two leather strips passed through incisions near the back.

Appreciating our author's contributions to the history of his time and place, it is a bit disconcerting to find the printed text of his book, so widely read for nearly two centuries, so frequently quoted by later historians and annalists and so generally conceded to be the authoritative account, differing in many particulars from his original manuscript, apparently his printer's copy. This, stitched into pamphlet form and bearing the names of several descendants, was found in the Manuscript Division of the Library of Congress. It was earlier in the possession of the historian Peter Force of Washington. The more important variations from the printed text disclosed by a careful line by line collation, are incorporated in the Notes of the present reprint. But only the more important; for so many and so various are the discrepancies, that their transcription would require more space than their interest warrants. Not only are there some differing spellings of places and persons, but many serious omissions of statement of fact; conversely there are found a few additions in the text seemingly added in proofreading, it may be by another hand. For it is not unlikely, in view of Penhallow's distance from Boston, or his inexperience in authorship, that Dr. Colman may have seen the book through the press; indeed, sentence structure where it has been changed and the occasional substitution of words of classical derivation for homely Anglo-Saxon, suggest the cultured Boston minister rather than the forceful Portsmouth merchant.

That the reader, if interested, may make the comparison for himself, a page of this original manuscript, selected more for its legibility than for the importance of its variations from the printed text, may be found reproduced in facsimile opposite page 38. It corresponds to that and the preceding page; about fifteen variations will be discovered. Whatever the explanation for these discrepancies, this study of the manuscript has revealed some hitherto unpublished history quite as interesting and important as that which got into the printed book.

Penhallow's book was reprinted for the first time in 1824, when the Publishing Committee of the New Hampshire Historical Society selected it for republication in the first volume of the Society's *Collections*. Though the *Indian Wars* had been printed only ninety-eight years previously, they noted the fact that it "had become so scarce, that it was with some trouble a complete copy could be found." They therefore sought the aid of "one of the most distinguished antiquaries of New England [Abiel Holmes,]" who, finding his own copy, used in preparing the *Annals*, imperfect, set about to secure a perfect copy. No one at the meeting of the Ameri-

INTRODUCTION.

can Academy, held at that time, could assist him to a copy. Harvard College Library had none, but he finally found one in the library of the Massachusetts Historical Society—entire, but "in great jeopardy,"—with loose leaves and title-page.

More than likely this may have been the very book used by Jeremy Belknap in the preparation of his *History of New Hampshire*, for in the year 1791,(*Proceedings* 1791, p.21), he had offered to give to the Society, in overpayment of his life membership fee of $34, among others, these three books—Penhallow's *Indian Wars*, Doolittle's *Narrative* (1750) and Norton's *Redeemed Captive* (1748), each today very scarce and very valuable. The Committee in reprinting, did not follow the old orthography or typographical style, but added "such notes as might serve to increase the value of the text." These excellent foot-notes also have been incorporated in the Notes of the present reprint.

In 1859 there appeared another reprint, if it may be so designated. It is a small quarto and its title-page bears a transcription of the original, not typographically faithful and with the following imprint: "Cincinnati:| Re-printed from the *Boston Edition of* 1726, with a *Memoir* and *Notes*, for W. Dodge,| by J. Harpel, corner Third| & Vine Sts.| 1859." But this is most decidedly *not* a reprint from the Boston edition of 1726. It is in fact a reprint *of the reprint* in the New Hampshire *Collections* of 1824. It has the typographical errors and, not invariably credited, the notes of this last. About twenty notes have

INTRODUCTION. xiii

been added. According to Allibone, this edition was privately printed and consisted of 150 copies. It has 129 pages, ending with Upham's poem taken from Farmer and Moore's *Collections*, I, p.35. Another form was issued, commonly called the second edition, preferred and more often seen, with a rubricated title-page but otherwise as the first, excepting that it bears a device, rubricated, (an Indian within a shield, with a legend) and the imprint is amended to read, "with a *Memoir, Notes*, and *Appendix*, for| Wm. Dodge . . ." In this issue, the 129 pages of the other are extended to 138, by selections from Farmer and Moore's *Collections*, Trumbull's *Indian Wars*, etc.; the added Appendix of 36 pages contains Gardener's *Pequot Wars*, and other excerpts.

Examples of still another issue were found. It has the rubricated title-page of the Cincinnati issue, but bears the following imprint: "Philadelphia:| . . . . . |by Oscar H. Harpel, P. T., [Qy. Professor of Typography?] Chestnut Street, 1859." Only two copies of this were discovered among eighty-five of the Cincinnati edition, of which seemingly it is merely a "freak" variant. So to, must be considered still another form bearing the imprint: "Boston, 1859."

Any enumeration of the extant copies of a rare book is necessarily tentative. One bibliographer compiled a list of known copies of the *Indian Wars*, a few years ago, in which appear the copy of the Library Company of Philadelphia and the one in the New York State Library, formerly in the Warden collection. This last has since been burned but the Philadelphia copy is known to have been stolen more than a half century ago. Such enumeration moreover should take into account the condition as well as the location of the book. It may be of interest to consider now the result of a more ambitious attempt to list the extant copies of the *Indian Wars*, completed after an exhaustive search in about a hundred American libraries most likely to contain the book and the scrutiny of many of the auction and sale catalogues issued during the last half century. Many of the books thus found have been examined carefully.

IMPERFECT COPIES RE-BOUND. Of these about a dozen are recorded. No more definite statement can be made, as the term "imperfect" is a relative one. As to condition some are not so very bad,—some are,—"title-page and last page in facsimile," "title-page and last three leaves in facsimile," "title-page mended and extended, three leaves from a shorter copy and last leaf in facsimile," "first twelve and last four leaves in manuscript"—and so they shade down to a few poor fragments, not worthy of consideration. Some of the defective surviving examples of the book started their circuit of the auction rooms more than a half century ago; by the peculiarity in the combination of their defects or of binding some may still be identified as they reappear catalogued from time to time. One, emerging from its concealment sixty years ago brought, in 1866, at its second sale, $35. After changing ownerships it sold, on its last appearance a few years ago for $600. Another imperfect copy, probably the one repeatedly offered in sale catalogues twenty years ago for $165, brought its owner, when it was last under the hammer, $975.

IMPERFECT COPIES IN ORIGINAL BINDING. Of these, ten were found, four in public libraries. Some are very imperfect. More than half of all imperfect examples of the book mourn the loss of the final leaf of Advertisement, for when the early reader had corrected "the great omission" on page 102, this nearly blank page served for a bit of writing-paper.

PERFECT COPIES RE-BOUND. Of the seven in this class, five are in public libraries, the sixth may be, and the remaining one is owned by the wealthiest of American book collectors and no doubt is destinated to public ownership. Several perfect and re-bound copies were offered in important English sale catalogues of many years ago. Some, if not all of these are most likely the identical ones here listed. At least they appear nowhere else.

PERFECT COPIES IN ORIGINAL BINDING. In other words: "collectors' copies." Five seems to be their number, two of which are in public libraries, two cannot be located, the remaining one is privately owned.

Thirty-seven perfect and fragmentary copies are thus accounted for. Of the twelve unmutilated examples of the book, seven are now in public libraries, five may or may not be hereafter purchasable.

In this reprint we have a well-executed photo-lithographic facsimile of a well preserved example of the book. The notes of the earlier editors, as well as those based on recent historical study and the addition of the more important unpublished material in the original manuscript, unknown to earlier students, appreciably enlarge the contents of the book as originally published. There has been added that which was sadly wanting for nearly two centuries—an important aid in the study of this source book—an Index.

EDWARD WHEELOCK.

THE HISTORY
OF THE
Wars of *New-England*,
With the *Eastern* Indians.
OR, A
NARRATIVE

Of their continued Perfidy and Cruelty,
from the 10th of *August*, 1703.
To the Peace renewed 13th of *July*, 1713.
And from the 25th of *July*, 1722.
To their Submission 15th *December*, 1725.
Which was Ratified *August* 5th 1726.

By *Samuel Penhallow*, Esqr.

*Nescio tu quibus es, Lector, lecturus Ocellis,
Hoc scio, quod siccis, scribere non potui.*

BOSTON:
Printed by *T. Fleet*, for *S. Gerrish* at the lower end of *Cornhill*, and *D. Henchman* over-against the Brick Meeting-House in *Cornhill*, 1726.

The Preface.

IT is one part of our Honour and Happiness in this Country, among the many difficulties and troubles which have attended the Settlements and growth of it unto this day, that there have not been wanting from time to time honest and worthy Persons, and some learned, who have delivered down to Posterity a plain and true account of the Wars which we have had with the Indian Natives in one part of the Land and in another.

We owe much unto Those who have done us this Service from the beginning, and they have herein served God, as well as obliged the World. For it always has been, and ever is like to be a grateful thing to Mankind to be informed of the rise and growth of Provinces, and of the sufferings of their feeble infant state: And from the days of Moses, who wrote the first History, the beginning of the World, and of Israel, the wise and pious among Men have scarce known a more sacred Pleasure, nor found a more profitable Entertainment, than in tracing the footsteps and windings of Divine Providence, in the planting of Colonies and Churches, here and there, thro' the Earth.

Nor let it seem vain in me to say, that in the settlement of the New-England Churches and Provinces, there have been some Circumstances so like unto those of Israel of old, (after their entrance into Canaan) that I am perswaded no People of God under Heaven, can sing of his Mercies and Judgments in the inspired Phrase

The PREFACE.

Phrase* *with more direct and pertinent self Application, than we can do.* The subject of the following Book *affords us the most special* Instance *hereof; Namely, that altho' our Merciful and Gracious God did in a wonderful manner,* cast out the Heathen *before our Fathers, and* Planted them; prepared also a room before them, and caused them to take deep root, and to fill the Land; *So that* the Vine hath sent out her Boughs unto the Sea, and her Branches upon the River; *Yet to* humbly and prove us, *and for our Sins to punish us, the Righteous* God hath left *a sufficient Number of the fierce and barbarous* Salvages *on our borders, to be* pricks in our Eyes, *and* thorns in our sides, *and they have been and are like the* Boar of the Woods to waste us, and the wild Beasts of the field to devour us.

Wherefore, on Principles both humane and religious, I gladly introduce the following Memoirs *to the publick view, with my hearty thanks to the* Honourable Author *for the great pains he has taken (among other his publick Services) to transmit these Particulars of the two last* Wars *with the Indian Enemy down to Posterity,* That the Generation to come might know them, and set their hope in God, and not forget his Works, but keep his Commandments.

The Reader *must not expect much Entertainment or Curiosity in the story of a* barbarous War *with cruel and perfidious* Salvages: *It is the benefit of* Posterity, *in a religious Improvement of this dry and bloody Story, that we aim at, in preserving some Remembrance thereof: And that in times to come, when we are dead and forgotten,* Materials may remain for a continued &

---

* 70 and 80 Psalms, and part of 105 106 and 107 Psalms.

The PREFACE.

entire History of our Country: *And we hope that they who come after us will take the like Care in their Times for the Children which shall be born.*

Let it suffice in praise of the Narrative, *if the Facts related be true and exact, and that the Style be familiar, plain and easy, as all* Historical Memoirs *should be writ. As to the Truth of it, none* (I suppose) *will have any doubt to whom the* Author *is known; and to whom among us is he not known? Or by whom among the lovers of the Country is he not esteemed for his affectionate regards unto the religious and civil Liberties of it?*

The Reverend Dr. Mather *wrote the* Remarkables of the Eastern War *before this, from the year* 1688. *unto the year* 1698. *ten years, wherefore he called his Book,* Decennium Luctuosum. *This Book may claim the like* Title, *for the first War here related, from* August *the* 10th 1703. *to the* 13th *of* July 1713. *did also continue just ten years.*

To these ten *years of Trouble and Distress the* Author *has added an Account of another but shorter War of three years, from* July 25. 1722. *to* December 15. 1725. *When the Salvages by their Delegates renew'd their Submission, and signed Articles of Peace in the Council-Chamber in* Boston; *for the lasting effects whereof we are humbly waiting on a Gracious* GOD *with our earnest Prayers. And we owe abundant* Praises *to his Holy Name for the great* Successes, *with which he has been pleased to crown the* Counsels *and* Arms *of the* Province *in this* last *short* War; *to the humbling the insolent Enemy and bringing them so soon to sue for the Peace which they had broken.* Not unto us, O LORD! not to us; but to thy Name give Glory; for thy Mercy and for thy Truth sake!

In

The PREFACE.

In a special manner, the wonderful Victory *obtained* August 12. 1724. *over the bold and Bloody* Tribe *at* Narridgwalk, *and their sudden Destruction that Memorable Day, was the singular Work of* GOD; *And the* Officers *and Soldiers piously put far from themselves the Honour of it. The plain hand of* Providence *and not their own* Conduct facilitated *and quickned their March.* God *sent 'em timely* Information *where the* Indians *had plac'd their Guards upon the River, that they might shun them, and so come upon the Town undiscovered.* God *brought them on it in a right time, when the fighting Men were just come in from abroad, and the next day (we are told) they were to have come down on our* Frontiers. *They were* surpris'd *in the height of security, and so* amaz'd *that they could not find their hands when they would have escaped. This Destruction of the Enemy was with the loss of only* one *life, and two wounded, on our part. And he who was the* Father *of the* War, *the* Ghostly Father *of those perfidious* Salvages, *like* Balaam the Son of Beor, *was* slain *among the Enemy, after his vain Endeavours to* Curse *us.*

May those singular Favours *of* GOD *have their* saving Effects *on us! and his* goodness *to us in the present fruits of* Peace *which we are about to reap* lead us to Repentance, *bind us to* Obedience, *raise us in* Devotion, *and endear his blessed Name and Truths and Ways to us.* Amen.

BENJAMIN COLMAN.

Boston, *Jan.* 28.
1725-.6.

The Introduction.

THE keeping a *Register of Memorable Occurrences*, as it has been the practice of former Ages, so it ought to be continued for the advantage of Posterity: And in as much as the *Divine Providence* has placed me near the Seat of Action, where I have had greater Opportunities than many others of remarking the Cruelty and Perfidy of the *Indian* Enemy, I thought it my Duty to keep a Record thereof. Not that at first I design'd to make these *Memoirs* publick but now am perswaded to it by some whose Judgment I pay a deference unto. In the collecting them, I have us'd all faithfulness; and have been assisted therein not only from the Abstracts of Original Letters, but from Persons of the best Credit and Reputation, and yet doubtless some small Occurences may have slipt my knowledge.

I might with *Orosius* very justly entitle this History *De miseria hominum*, being no other then a Narrative of *Tragical Incursions* perpetrated by Bloody *Pagans*, who are Monsters of such Cruelty, that the words of *Virgil* may not unaptly be apply'd to them.

Tristius haud illis monstrum, nec Sævior ulla
Pestis et ira Deum.

Who are as implacable in their Revenge, as they are terrible in the Execution of it; and will convey it down to the third and fourth Generation. No Courtesy will ever oblige them to gratitude; for their greatest Benefactors have frequently fall'n as Victims to their Fury.

The *Roman Spectacles* of old were very lively in them

Introduction.

them tepeated. God has made them a terrible Scourge for the punishment of our Sins. And probably that very Sin of ours in neglecting the welfare of their *Souls*. For *we* have not expressed the like laudable Care for them, as hath been done in the *Southern* and *Western* parts of the Country. But indeed we have rather aimed to advance a private Trade, then to instruct them in the Principles of true Religion. This brings to my remembrance a remarkable saying of one of their Chief *Sachems*, whom (a little before the War broke out) I asked, Wherefore it was they were so much bigoted to the *French*? Considering their Traffick with them was not so advantageous as with the *English*. He gravely reply'd, *That the Friars taught them to Pray, but the English never did*.

And it is also remarkably observable that among all the *Settlements* and *Towns* of Figure and Distinction, not one of them have been utterly destroy'd where ever a *Church* was gathered.

But if the *Eastern parts* have been remiss, this should no ways detract from the praise of that incomparable zeal of the Venerable Mr. *Elliot*, and the indefatigable Pains which the renowned Mr. *Mayhew*, and others, have exercised in the Instruction and Conversion of the *Natives* in their parts: wherein they were so far Successful (thro' the Blessing of God) as to form many Churches of Baptiz'd *Indians*; and to gather many Assemblys of *Catechumens*, that profess the Name of *Christ*; which remain to this day the Fruit and Reward of their Labours, will bespeak their *Praise* to future Ages, and the *Thanksgiving of many* to GOD.

S. P.

THE HISTORY
Of the Wars of *New-England*, &c.

IT is ſtoried of *Tiſſaphernes*, That ſo ſoon as he entred into a League with *Ageſilaus* King of *Sparta*, he ſtudied means whereby to infringe and violate the ſame: Upon which *Ageſilaus* ſent his Ambaſſadors unto him to return him Thanks, that by ſo doing he had made the Gods his Enemies. Now conſidering the League that has been ſolemnized with the *Indians*, together with their Cruelty and Treachery ſo notoriouſly perpetrated, it's no wonder if in the ſequel of this Hiſtory, we find them under ſome ſignal Remark of the Divine Diſpleaſure.

NOT that I am unsensible that many have stigmatiz'd the *English* as chiefly culpable in causing the first Breach between them and us; by invading their Properties, and defrauding them in their Dealings: But to censure the Publick for the sinister Actions of a few private Persons, is utterly repugnant to Reason and Equity. Especially considering the great Care that the *Legislative* Power had taken to protect the *Natives*, and their Interests.

WHAT hath formerly occur'd of this kind is none of my business to discant upon here; but as to the Infraction which I am about to make mention of, I never yet heard the least Word in their favour, but all sorts of Persons do condemn their Perfidy

AT the arrival of Governour *Dudley* in the Year 1702. the whole Body of *Indians* was in a tolerable good Frame and Temper; but being animated by the *French*, they soon began to threaten and insult the *English*: Upon which in the succeeding Year *June* the 20th. a *Congress* was appointed at *Casco,* where the Chiefs of the several *Tribes* met,

viz. *Mauxus,* and *Hopehood* from *Naridgewalk, Wanungunt,* & *Wanadugunbuent* from *Penobscot, Wattanamunton, Adiawando* and *Hegen* from *Pennecook,* and *Pigwacket.*

Mesambomett, and *Wexar,* from *Amasconty,* with about 250 Men in 65 Canoos, well arm'd, and mostly *painted* with variety of Colours, which seemingly were affable and kind, and yet in some Instances gave cause of jealousy.

A *Tent* being fixt for entertaining the *Governour*
and

and Gentlemen who accompanied him, together with the *Sagamores*; His Excellency very kindly saluted them, saying, "That as he was Commissionated by the Great and Victorious *Queen* of *England*, he came to visit them as his *Friends* and *Brethren*, and to reconcile whatever Differences had hapned since the last *Treaty*."

AT this they made a pause, but after a short Intermission Captain *Simmo*, who was their Orator arose, and said, "That they acknowledged his Favour in giving them a Visit at such a juncture, with so many of the *Council* and Gentlemen of both *Provinces*; assuring him, that they aimed at nothing more than *Peace*; and that as high as the *Sun* was above the Earth, so far distant should their Designs be of making the least breach between each other" And as a Testimony thereof they presented him a Belt of *Wampam*, and invited him to the *Two Pillars* of Stones, which at a former Treaty were erected, and called by the significant Name of the TWO BROTHERS; unto which both Parties went, and added a greater Number of Stones.

THIS Ceremony being performed, several Volleys were discharged on each side; and the *Indians* added their usual dancing, singing, and loud acclamations of Joy. *Trading-houses* in several places were hereupon engaged; and that the Price of Commodities should be stated, and an *Armourer* fixed at the publick Charge. Many *Presents* were also made them, which they kindly received; so that every thing lookt with a promising Aspect of a settled Peace: And that which afterward seem'd to confirm it, was the coming in of Captain *Bomaseen*, and Captain *Samuel*, who informed, that several *Missionaries* from the *Fryars* were lately come among them, who endeavoured to break the Union, and seduce them from their Allegiance to the Crown of *England*; but had made no Impression on them, for that they were *as firm as the Mountains*, and should continue so, as long as the Sun and Moon endured.

THE *Eastern* Inhabitants, who before had thoughts of removing, were now encouraged to stand their Ground; several more were also preparing to settle among them, partly from the fertility of the Soil, the plenty of Timber, the advantage of Fishery, and several other Inducements. But I should have taken notice of *two* Instances in the late Treaty, wherein the matchless Perfidy of these bloody Infidels did notoriously appear. 1*st*. As the Treaty was concluded with Volleys on both sides, as I said before, the *Indians* desired the *English* to fire first, which they readily did, concluding it no other but a Complement; but so soon as the *Indians* fired, it was observ'd that their Guns were charg'd with Bullets; having contrived (as was afterwards confirm'd) to make the *English* the Victims of that Day. But Providence so order'd it, as to place their chief Counsellours and *Sachems* in the Tent where ours were seated, by which means they could not destroy one without endangering the other! 2. As the *English* waited some Days for *Watanummon* (the *Pigwacket Sachem*) to compleat their Council, it was afterward discovered, that they only tarried for a Reinforcement of 200 *French* and *Indians*, who in three Days after we

returned

returned came among them; having resolved to seize the Governour, Council and Gentlemen, and then to Sacrifice the Inhabitants at pleasure; which probably they might have done, had they not been prevented by an overuling Power.

But notwithstanding this Disappointment, they were still resolved on their bloody *Design*: For within six Weeks after the whole *Eastern* Country was in a Conflagration, no House standing, nor Garrison unattackt. *August* 10th at nine in the Morning they began their bloody *Tragedy*, being about five hundred *Indians* of all sorts, with a number of *French*; who divided themselves into several Companies, and made a Descent on the several Inhabitants from *Casco* to *Wells* at one and the same time, sparing none of every Age or Sex.

AS the milk white Brows of the Grave and *Ancient* had no respect shown; so neither had the mournful cries of tender *Infants* the least pity; for they triumph'd at their Misery, and applauded such as the skilfullest Artists, who were most dexterous in contriving the greatest Tortures; which was enough to turn the most *Stoical Apathie* into Streams of mournful Sympathy and Compassion.

THE Town of *Wells*, which valiantly stood its Ground both in the former and latter War, suffered now great Spoil, nor could escape without the loss of 39 that were kill'd and taken.

Cape-Porposs being inhabited only by a few Fishermen, was wholly laid desolate. But the Garrison at *Winter-Harbour* defended itself with much Bravery; yet it was at last overpowered by by Force, and then submitted on Terms

Saco Fort was also attackt by the Enemy with great Fury; they kill'd eleven, and carried twenty four Captive.

Spurwink, which was principally inhabited by the *Jordans*, had no less than twenty two of that Family kill'd and taken.

THOSE at *Scarborough* were mostly in Garrison, whom the *Indians* not willing to encounter, sent a *Captive* before with a Flag of Truce; but the *Officer* being acquainted with their Intreagues, slighted the Message, secured the Captive, and made a vigorous Defence. However, by a long Siege they were so reduced, that had not Recruits been sent them, they had utterly been overthrown.

Perpooduck was of all places (for number) the greatest sufferers, being but nine Families, and no Garrison to retire unto; neither any Men at home, where they took eight, and inhumanly butchered twenty five; among whom was the Wife of *Michael Webber*, who being big with Child, they knockt her on the head, and ript open her Womb, cutting one part of the Child out; a Spectacle of horrid Barbarity.

Casco, which was the utmost Frontier, commanded by Major *March*, who was all this while unsensible of the Spoil that the *Indians* had done, was saluted by *Mauxis*, *Wanungonet*, and *Affacombuit*, three of their most vallant and puissant *Sachems*. They gradually advanced with a Flag of Truce, and sent one before them to signify that they had matter of moment to impart to him.

him. At first he flighted the Message, but on second Thoughts went out to meet them; they seeming to him but few in number, and unarmed: However he ordered two or three Sentinels to be ready in case of Danger. Their Voice to him at first seem'd like the Voice of *Jacob*, but their Hands were like the Hands of *Esau*: *With their Tongues they used deceit, and the Poison of Asps was under their Lips*. For no sooner had they saluted him, but with Hatchets under their Mantles they violently assaulted him; having a number that lay in Ambush near them, who shot down one of his Guards: But being a Person of uncommon Strength, as well as Courage, he soon wrested a Hatchet from one of them, with which he did good Execution: Yet if Sergeant *Hook* (with a file of Ten from the Fort) had not speedily succoured him, they would soon have overpowered him. Mr. *Phippeny* and Mr. *Kent*, who accompanied him, were attackt by others, and soon fell by their Fury; for being advanced in Years, they were so infirm, that I might say of them as *Juvenal* did of *Priam*, They had scarce Blood enough left to tinge the Knife of the Sacrifice.

THE Enemy being defeated in this their Design, fell upon the several Cottages which lay round, and destroyed all they could. But the Major on rallying his Men together, seeing nothing but Fire and Smoak, divided them into three parts, which were twelve in each, and interchanged them every two Hours, who thus continued six Days and Nights without the least Intermission; by which time the whole Body of

Indians

Indians came together, being upwards of five hundred, besides *French* commanded by Monsieur *Bobasser*, who had ransackt and laid waste the several Settlements before-mentioned; and being flusht with Success, having taken one Sloop, two Shallops, and much Plunder, attempted to undermine the Fort from the Water side in which they proceeded two Days and Nights, and probably would have effected their Design, if they had not been prevented by the arrival of Capt. *Southack*, who raised the siege, retook the Shallop, and shattered their *Navy*, which was upward of 200 *Cannoos*.

ON *Tuesday* after Capt. *Tom*, with thirty *Indians*, made a descent on *Hampton* Village, where they slew four, besides the Widow *Mussey*, who was a remarkable speaking *Quaker*, and much lamented by that Sect. They also rifled two Houses near the Garrison, but fearing a pursuit, drew off; it being generally observed, that they seldom annoy but by surprize.

BY this time Capt. *Summersby* was ordered with his Troop to *Portsmouth*, and Capt. *Wadley* to *Wells* with the like Company of *Dragoons*; many concluding that the *Eastern* parts would be the seat of Action; and yet a few Days after, Advice was brought from *Deerfield*, (as a forerunner of some greater Evil) of two Men taken and carried to *Canada*; which so alarm'd the Country, to see the Frontiers insulted two hundred Miles in length, that on *September* 26th. the Governour ordered 360 Men to *Pigwacket*, one of their principal Head-quarters: But thro' the difficulty of the Passage, and unskilfulness of the Guides,

Guides, they return'd without any Discovery.

Capt. *Davis* at the same time had the like misfortune, who went to the Ponds, but it seem'd the Enemy went *Eastward*: For on the 6th. of *October*, Capt. *Hunnuell* with nineteen Men, as they were going to work in their Meadows at *Blackpoint*, were way-laid by two hundred *Indians*, who at one stroke kill'd and took the whole body Excepting one, who like *Job's Messenger* was preserved to give the Melancholy Account thereof. Upon this they attack't the *Fort*, where only Eight Men were left under the Command of Lieu. *Wyat*, who by the encouragement of Capt. *Willard*, and Capt. *Wells*, that were there in two Sloops stood their Ground some time, but being afterward dispirited they went on board Capt. *Wells*, and the Enemy set the deserted Garrison on fire.

Another Company of *Indians* commanded by *Sampson* fell on *York*, where they slew *Arthur Brandon*'s Wife and five Children, carrying Captive with them the Widow *Parsons* and her Daughter.

The former attempt on *Pigwackett* proving unsuccessful, Collonel *March* went a second time with the like number of Men, where he kill'd six *Indians* and took as many more with some plunder, which was the *first Reprisal* that we made; but the Enemy dispersing into small parties, did much more mischief then in larger; which put the Country into a far greater Confusion, in somuch that there was no safety to him that went out, nor unto him that came in, but dreadful Calamity on every side:

C —*Ter-*

―――― *Terror ubique tremor* ――――

At *Berwick* they ambusht five, and as the store Ship was entring *Casco*, they entertained them so unexpectedly with a Volley of Shot, that the Master with three more were Slain, and two in the Boat wounded.

The *General Assembly* being sensibly affected with the state of matters, and dispos'd to a Vigorous prosecution of the War, enacted, That *Forty Pounds* should be given for every *Indian Scalp*, which prompted some, and animated others to a noble Emulation. Capt. *Ting* was the first that embraced the tender, who in the depth of Winter, went to their head quarters, and got five, for which he received two hundred Pounds. Major *Hilton* also with five Companies more made the like Essay, and so did Capt. *Stephens*, but returned with no other Lawrel than the safety of themselves and Company.

The Enemy went on daring and succesful. They frequently followed the tracts of our Men in their Marches: At *Berwick* they kill'd one, wounded another, and burnt two Houses. After that they made a descent on *Andrew Neals* Garrison, where they were vigorously repuls'd by Capt. *Brown*, who kill'd nine on the spot and wounded many more, which so enraged those Wretches, that at their return they executed their revenge on *Joseph Ring* who was then a Captive among them, whom they fastned to a Stake and burnt alive; barbarously shouting and rejoycing at his cries.

February 8th. *Joseph Bradleys* Garrison of *Haverhil* was unhappily surpriz'd by a small Scout, who sculking at a distance, and seeing the

Gates

(11)

Gates open and none on the Sentry, rushed in and became Masters thereof. The *Housewife* perceiving the Misery that was attending her, and having boiling Soap on the Fire, scalded one of them to Death. The Sentinel within was slain, and she with several others were taken; which was the second time of her Captivity. But that which heightned her Affliction was being with Child, and yet oblig'd to travel in a deep Snow, under a heavy Burden, and many Days together without Subsistance, excepting a few bits of Skin, Ground-nuts, Bark of Trees, wild Onions, and Lilly Roots. Nevertheless she was wonderfully supported, and at last safely delivered; but the Babe soon perisht for want of Nourishment, and by the Cruelty of the *Indians*, who as it cry'd, threw hot Embers in its Mouth. After a Years Bondage she was sold to the *French* for eighty Livers, and then redeemed by her Husband.

THE Use of *Snow-shoes* appearing very requisite for marching in the Winter Season, occasioned an Act in both *Provinces* for supplying the Frontiers therewith: And this Season, which before was dreaded as most hazardous, was now the time of greatest safety, and of less difficulty in travelling.

BUT the *Southern* Parts not thinking themselves in so much Danger, did in a little time become secure, which the Enemy taking notice of, fell on *Deerfield*, of which the Reverend Mr. *Stoddard* gave me the following Account. That Collonel *Schuyler*, who was always a kind and faithful Intelligencer, gave timely warning thereof, which awaken'd some, but was slighted by others.

others: However, Mr. *Williams*, the worthy Pastor of that Place, was strongly possest that the Town would in a little time be destroyed; signifying as much in his publick Ministry, and private Conference; and could not be satisfied till he had got twenty Soldiers to be posted there. A few Nights before the Assault was, they were strangely amused, by a trampling Noise round the Fort, as if it were beset by *Indians*. Towards Morning, being *February* 29th. the Enemy sent Scouts to discover the posture of the Town, who observing the Watch walking in the Streets, returned and put them to a stand: A while after they sent again, and were advised, that all was then still and quiet: Upon which, two hours before Day, they attackt the Fort, and by the advantage of some drifts of Snow, got over the Walls. The whole Body was above two hundred and fifty, under the Command of Monsieur *Arteil*, who found the People fast asleep and easily secured them. The most considerable part of the Town thus fell into their Hands. They left no Garrison unattackt, excepting that of Capt. *Wells* ; But at *Benoni Stebbins*'s they met with some repulse, and lost several. Sixty of the *English* fell, whereof many were stifled in a Celler; and a hundred were taken Captive, who with a melancholly Countenance condoled each other's Misery, yet durst not express the Anguish of their Souls. That Day and Night were spent in plundering, burning and destroying. The next Morning they withdrew into the Woods, carrying with them their Plunder and Captives; among whom was the Reverend Mr. *Williams*,
(before

(before mentioned) whose Sufferings, with his Neighbours, through a deep Snow, over mountainous Desarts, were exceeding great; besides many Trials and Fears which they laboured under.

The Country being alarm'd, several hastned to their Relief; about thirty of those which first came, charged the Enemy in the rear, and being strengthned with a farther Supply, pursued them with good Success; but the Enemy returning, and being much superiour in Number, kill'd nine of ours in the Skirmish.

The Day after there was a considerable Confluence from the lower Towns, as well as from the County of *Hartford*, but for want of *Snowshoes*, were unable to pursue them. Some of our Captives then in *Canada*, knowing the Enterprize that was on Foot, sent several Letters unto their Friends, which the Enemy did carefully put into a Bag, and hung it upon the limb of a Tree in the high-way; which Letters were afterwards found, and gave Satisfaction of those that were then alive among them.

While the *Indians* by Land were every way distressing of us, the *French* by Sea were as industrious to impoverish us.

April 7th. 1704. they fitted out a *Privateer Shallop* with twenty seven Men, to intercept our *Southern* Trade as they came laden with Provisions; which if they had succeeded in, would not only have supplied their own indigent Forces, but the *Indians* also; (who were then forming a desperate Design against us) But thro' the favour of God to us, they were cast away on *Plimouth* Shore.

Shore. A like signal Favour to us was the taking a *Store-Ship* of theirs (by our *Virginia* Fleet) of Forty Guns, bound to *Canada*, in which were twenty Officers, two thousand small Arms, with Ammunition answerable; besides a vast number of Crucifixes, and Presents of a greater value for encouraging the *Indians* in acts of Hostility against the *English*. In the Engagement their General was slain, the only Man that fell in Battle, by whose Interest those *Stores* were procured; which loss was so affecting, that (as some of our Captives afterwards reported) it caused a deep Humiliation throughout *Canada* a considerable time after.

As the Spring advanced, it was thought necessary to guard the Frontiers with fresh Troops, upon which Major *Mason* with ninety five of the *Pequod,* and *Mohegan* Indians were posted at *Berwick*, who at first were very terrifying to the Enemy: Yet frequent assaults were afterwards made at a little Distance, as on *April* 25th. *Nathaniel Meador* was shot while at work in his Field. They mangled his dead Corps after a barbarous manner. Next day they kill'd *Edward Taylor* near *Lampreel River*, and after that took his *Wife* and *Son* whom they carried to *Canada*, and she was afterwards redeemed. From thence they went to *Cochecho,* expecting to have made Mr. *Waldron* the Victim of that Day; but being happily from home, they miss't their aim. However they surpriz'd a Servant of his, as she went to the Well for Water, whom (after they had examined concerning her Master, the State of the Garrison, and other Affairs) they knockt on the head, but

but the Stroke not proving fatal, she afterwards recovered.

After this several were assaulted in the Road to *Wells*, whereof two were kill'd, one taken, and another made his Escape.

May 13th. an Express came from *North Hampton*, advising, that about break of Day a Company of *French* and *Indians*, fell on a fortified House at *Pascomuck*, where no watch being kept, the People were alarm'd in their beds by the noise of the Enemy's rushing on the house ; and before the Inhabitants could rise, the *Indians* had got their Guns thro' the *Port-holes*, and shot those that first appeared, killing some and wounding others. The surprized People made what resistance they could, firing briskly on the Enemy ; but the house being soon set on fire, they were forc'd to yield themselves Prisoners. The Enemy soon drew off, but fearing a pursuit, dismist one of the wounded, with this Caution, that if the *English* followed them they would Slay the Prisoners, but the unfortunate Messenger in returning back was Slain by another *Indian*. On the same Morning another Party attacked a Farm house two Miles off, but the fury of the Dogs so alarm'd the Inhabitants, that they instantly got up and fired several Guns to very good advantage, which prevented any further attempt. As for those at *Pascomuck* they were immediatly pursued, three made an Escape, eight were rescued, nineteen slain, & three carryed to *Canada*. Next day Major *Whitting*, pursued them with a number of Horses, and came upon their Track, but the Ways were so impassible, that they sent their Horses back with, a resolve to follow them on Foot, but some proving lame, and others tyring, caused the rest to desist. I would here remark, that a little before the Troubles at *Pascomuck*, and the Farm house before mentioned, the People at *Springfield* heard a great shooting; Unto some it seem'd to be at *Westfield*, to others at a *Village*, and to some again in the *Woods*; so that many hastned to their assistance; but when they came all was still and quiet, the reason whereof is hard to assign, and yet we have repeated instances in History of the like nature.

Under all those Sufferings from a cruel Enemy little or no impression could ever be made by us upon them, by reason of their retiring into unaccessable Swamps, and Mountains. Wherefore it was determined, that Major *Church*, who was so eminently Serviceable in the former War, should visit their head quarters, according to a *Scheme* which he had projected.

No sooner was his Commission granted, but he rais'd a considerable number of *Volunteers* out of *Plimouth* Colony both of *English* and *friend Indians*, and marched to *Nantaskett* for further Instructions; where the following Gentlemen were appointed Officers under him. *viz*. Colonel *Goreham*, Major *Hilton*, Capt. *John Brown, Constant,* & *Edward Church, Cole, Dyer, Lamb, Cook, Harreden, Williamson,* and *Myrick*, with five hundred and fifty Men in fourteen *Transports*, and with thirty six *Whaleboats*, which were guarded by Capt. *Smith, Rogers,* and *Southack*, in three ships of War. After they were equipt, they sail'd to *Piscataqua*, to make up their Compliment from thence. May 15th.

15th. they sail'd Eastward, visiting all parts as they went along, till they came to the Green Islands, where they took Monsieur *Lafebure*, and his two Sons with a *Canada Indian*, whom they examined apart: The Father at first seem'd Surly and Crooked, and the young Men were much of the like Temper, but being told what they must trust unto in case they did not confess, were afterwards Submissive, and promis'd to Pilot them where ever they were directed. Upon this the Transports and Whaleboats were ordered to be in a readiness, and every Man to have a weeks Provision; From hence they paddled to *Penobscot*, and with the assistance of one *D' Young*, whom they bro't out of *Boston* Goal on purpose for a Pilot, kill'd and took a considerable number both of *French* and *Indians*, among whom was St. *Casteen*'s Daughter. From thence they went to *Passamaquada*, and *Mount Desart*, where they met the three Ships of War according to Appointment. Their Custom was to rest in the Day, and row in the Night; and never to fire at an *Indian* if they could reach him with a Hatchet, for fear of allarming them. Here they siez'd the Old *Lotriell* and his Family, after that Mounsier *Guorden*, and *Sharkee*, who a little before came with a Comission from *Canada* to form an Expedition against the *English*. No sooner had our Forces arrived here, but Orders were sent them from *Boston*, forthwith to Sail to *Port-Royall*, expecting some store Ships from *France*, which was welcome News for Officers & Soldiers. But they miss'd of their Expectations: However the Ships stood off the Harbour while the Land Forces went to *Menn*, where a Council

D   cil

cil of War was held, and Lievt. *Giles* was sent to the Town with a Flag of Truce and Summons to Surrender; Their Anfwer was, "*That If our forces would not hurt their Eftates they would Surrender, otherwife were refolved to ftand their ground.* Upon which a defcent was made upon them that Night, but little effected until the Morning, and then the Forces drew up and drove all before them.

There was at this time a confiderable plenty of Brandy, and Clarret in their Houfes, which rather proved a fnare than fervice to our Men; Efpecially the *Indians*, who naturally affect ftrong Drink, but this was foon prevented, by breaking in the heads of the Casks. Lieutenant *Baker* and one more were kill'd in this Attack, and not above fix died in the whole Expedition. Moft of their Houfes were burnt, and much Plunder taken, but with as little Effufion of Blood as poffibly could be. The *General* ordered their Damms to be dug down, and their Fortifications to be laid in Afhes. Having as great fuccefs as reafonably could be expected, thro' out all the Territorys of *L' Accadia*, and *Nova Scotia*, where he took a hundred Prifoners, burnt and laid waft all the *French* Settlements, (except the Town of *Port Royal*) a great many Cattle were alfo kill'd, and the *Indians* driven into fuch Confufion, that they left their Wigwams and retired into private Cells.

ON *July* 4th. a Council of War was call'd to concert what next to do, who refolved, that as the Fort was alarm'd, the Enemy was more numerous than at firft; and that as many of our Men

were

were tyred and defective, it would be best to return; which was also consented unto by our Sea-Officers. But notwithstanding the Fatigue that this worthy *Gentleman* had undergone, and the Dangers he had run; the Spoil he had done, and the Victories he wan, yet he could not escape the Censures of many. Some indeed extol'd his Valour and Conduct even to an *Hyperbole*, while others endeavoured to lessen it with as much Disgrace and Infamy. Some thought he did too much, others too little: But after one and another had pass'd their Sentiments, the *General Assembly* (which was then sitting) voted him *Thanks for the good Services he did both to the* Queen *and* Country.

The Governour of *Port-Royal* being in fear of a new Enterprize, sent *Lewis Allein* as a Spy, under the Colour of a *Flag of Truce*, with six Prisoners, (whereof Mr *Hoddy* of *Piscataqua* was one) to observe and know the Motion of the *English*. But being suspected, he was apprehended and searcht, and in his Pocket-book was found this Direction; *That if any Enterprize was on foot, he should (in his* Advice-book*) joyn* L. A. *the two first Letters of his Name, close together; if it was only in Agitation, to place them at some Distance; but if nothing was in Motion, then to sign a* Cross.

While our Forces were engaged in visiting the Enemy abroad, great care was taken of covering the Frontiers at home; and yet very daring Assaults were frequently made by small numbers. At *Oyster-River* they wounded *William Tasket*, and at *Dover* they way-laid the Inhabitants as they returned from publick Worship: After that they kill'd.

kill'd a Lad near *Casco* Fort. About the same time some of the Enemy were Fishing up *Connecticut* River, and being trackt by a small Scout of our Volunteers, one *Englishman* and five *Mohegen Indians*, they pursued them to such advantage, that they slew the whole Company, save one, which were nine in number. Mr. *Caleb Lyman*, (now *Elder* of a Church in *Boston*) was Leader in this hardy Action, and has favoured us with the following Account of it.

Mr. Caleb Lyman's *Account of Eight Enemy Indians kill'd by himself, and five Friend Indians,*

SOme time in the Month of *May*, 1704. there came Intelligence from *Albany*, of a number of Enemy *Indians* up *Connecticut* River, who had built a Fort, and planted Corn, at a place called *Cowassuck*. On the fifth of *June* following, we set out (by order of Authority) from *Northampton*, and went nine Days Journey into the Wilderness, (thro' much Difficulty, by reason of the Enemy's Hunting and Scouting in the Woods, as we perceived by their Tracks and Firing) and then came across some fresh Tracks, which we followed till we came in sight of the abovesaid River: Supposing there might be a Number of *Indians* at hand; we being not far from the place where the Fort was said to be built. Here we made a Halt, to consult what Methods to take; and soon concluded to send out a Spy, with Green Leaves for a *Cap* and *Veste*, to prevent his own Discovery, and to find out the Enemy. But before our

Spy

Spy was gone out of sight, we saw two *Indians*, at a confiderable diftance from us, in a *Cannoo*, and fo immediately recall'd him: And foon after we heard the firing of a Gun up the River. Upon which we concluded to keep clofe till Sunfet; and then if we could make any further Difcovery of the Enemy, to attack them, if poffible, in the Night. And accordingly, when the Evening came on, we mov'd towards the River, and foon perceived a *Smoke*, at about half a Miles diftance, as we tho't, where we (afterwards) found they had taken up their Lodging. But fo great was the Difficulty, that (tho' we ufed our utmoft Care and Diligence in it) we were not able to make the approach till about *Two* a Clock in the Morning, when we came within Twelve Rods of the *Wigwam*, where they lay. But here we met with a new Difficulty, which we fear'd would have ruin'd the whole Defign: For the Ground was fo covered over with dry Sticks and Brufh, for the fpace of five Rods, that we cou'd not pafs, without making fuch a *Crackling*, as we tho't would alarm the Enemy, and give them Time to efcape. But while we were contriving to compafs our Defign, God in his good Providence fo ordered, that a very *fmall* Cloud arofe, which gave a fmart *Clap of Thunder*, and a fudden Shower of Rain. And this Opportunity we embraced, to run thorow the Thicket; and fo came undifcovered within fight of the *Wigwam*; and perceived by their Noife, that the Enemy were awake. But however, being unwilling to lofe any Time, we crept on our Hands and Knees till we were within three or four Rods of them.

them. Then we arose, and ran to the side of the *Wigwam*, and *fired* in upon them: And flinging down our *Guns*, we surrounded them with our *Clubs* and *Hatchets*, and knockt down several we met with. But after all our Diligence, *Two* of their Number made their escape from us: One *mortally* wounded, and the other not hurt; as we afterwards heard.

When we came to look over the slain, we found *seven* dead upon the spot: *Six* of whom we *scalpt*, and left the other unscalpt. (Our *Indians* saying, They would give *one* to the Country, since we had each of us one; and so concluded we should all be rich eno') When the Action was thus over, we took our *Scalps* and *Plunder*; such as *Guns*, *Skins*, &c. and the Enemies *Canoos*; in which we came down the River about twelve Miles, by break of Day; and then tho't it Prudence to dismiss and break the *Canoos*; knowing there were some of the Enemy betwixt us and Home.

And now all our Care being, how to make a safe and comfortable Return, we first lookt over our Provision, and found we had not more than eno' for one small Refreshment: and being above one hundred Miles from any *English* Settlement, we were very tho'tful how we shou'd subsist by the way. For having trackt about *Thirty* of the Enemy a little before us, we could not *hunt* for our Subsistance, for fear of Discovery: And so were obliged to eat *Buds of Trees*, *Grass*, & *Strawberry Leaves*, for the space of four or five Days, til, thro' the goodness of God, we safely arrived at *Northampton*, on the 19th or 20th of the aforesaid

said *June*. And some time after (upon our humble Petition to the *Great and General Court*, to consider the Service we had done) we received *Thirty one Pounds* Reward. And I have only this to observe, that in Consequence of this Action, the Enemy were generally alarm'd, and immediately forsook their Fort and Corn at *Cowassuck*, and never return'd to this Day, that we cou'd hear of, to renew their Settlement in that place.

I beg the *Country's* leave to observe, How *poorly* this bold Action, and great Service was rewarded: No doubt they looked for, and well deserved, *eight* times as much; and *now* the *Province* would readily pay eight hundred pounds in the like Case: But a gracious God has recompenced to the *Elder*, I trust, both in the Blessings of his Providence and Grace.

The *French* in *Canada* were now forming another design on *North Hampton*, of which we had Seasonable Advice; Yet two Men were kill'd going to *Deerfield*. After that came in a *French* deserter, who informed of the State of the Army that was then coming: Upon this, Expresses & Scouts were every way sent to observe their Motion; Major *Whiting* with a considerable Number went to the Ponds, where he expected to give them Battle, but they were gone from thence, leaving their Cannoos behind, which he burnt. Their whole Body were seven hundred, with two *Fryers*, under the Command of Mounsieur *Boocore*, who in their March began to Muting about the Plunder, which they had in View & expected to be master off: Forgetting the Proverb

verb about dividing the Skin before the Bear was kill'd. Their Diſſention at laſt was ſo great, that upwards of two hundred return'd in diſcontent. However the reſt came on, and ſent Scouts before to obſerve the Poſture of the *Engliſh*, who reported, that they were as thick as the Trees in the Woods. Upon which their Spirits fail'd, & more of their number deſerted. They then call'd a Council of War, who reſolved to deſiſt from the Enterprize. Yet ſome ſtaid, and afterwards fell on *Lancaſter*, and *Groaton*, where they did ſome Spoil, but not what they expected, for that theſe Towns were ſeaſonably ſtrengthened.

 Capt. *Ting* and Capt. *How* entertained a warm diſpute with them for ſome time, but being much inferiour in Number, were forced to retreat with ſome loſs; yet thoſe that were Slain of the Enemy, were more then thoſe of ours. One of them was an Officer of ſome Diſtinction, which ſo Exaſperated their Spirits, that in revenge they fired the Meeting Houſe, kill'd ſeveral Cattle, and burnt many Out-houſes. About the ſame time Capt. *Allen* from *Weſtfield* diſcovered a ſmall Partie with whom he had a Skirmiſh, and loſt one Man, but kill'd three, and reſcued a Captive. After this, between *Hadley* and *Quabaug*, we had one wounded and another Slain. By this time came Major *Tailor* with his Troop, (who always diſtinguiſh't himſelf of an active Spirit to ſerve his Country) Capt. *Preſcot*, *Buckley*, and *Willard* with their Companies, who were ſo vigorous and intenſe in purſuing the Enemy, that they put them all to flight. And yet a little while after they fell on *Groaton*, and *Naſhaway*, where they

kill'd

kill'd Lieut. *Wyler*, and several more. It was not then known how many of the Enemy were slain, it being customary among them to carry off their Dead: However it was afterward affirm'd, that they lost sixteen besides several that were wounded. After this they divided into smaller Parties, and did much Mischief, as at *Aimsbury*, *Haverhil*, and *Exeter*. *August* 11th. they wounded *Mark Giles* of *Dover*, (with his Son) who thro' anguish of Pain, and much effusion of Blood, expired a few days after. At the same time another Partie fell on *York*, where they slew *Matthew Austin* near the Garrison, and then went to *Oyster River*, where they kill'd several while at Work in their Field.

The five Nations of *Indians* which are called by the Name of the *Oneydes*, *Onnondages*, *Cayonges*, *Senneches*, and *Macquaus*, all this while stood Neuter: But being like to be influenced by the *French Missionaries* who came among them, Colonel *Townsend* and Mr. *Leverett* from the *Massachusetts*, Capt. *Gold* and Capt. *Levinston* from *Connecticut*, were Commissionated to give them a Visit, and strengthen the Alliance with them; which they did to so good Effect, that they promis'd to take up the *Hatchet*, whenever the Governour of *New-York* should desire it. But why so fair an Opportunity was lost, when the Interest of *New-England* lay bleeding, was matter of Surprize and Admiration to some, of Censures and Reflections to others. The only Account we can give of it is, the vast Trade between the *Dutch* and *Indians*; for the sake of which, that Government have always chosen to restrain their *Indians* from joyning

ing with us in our Wars. In the midſt of War, there ſeems a ſecret League between them and the Governour of *Canada*, not to ſuffer the leaſt breach to be made on one another by any of their *Indians*.

But although my Deſign was only to remark the barbarous Inſults of thoſe bloody Pagans on the Territories of *New-England*; yet I think it not improper to take a ſhort view of their Deſcent on *Newfoundland*, conſidering the nearneſs of its Scituation, and that ſeveral of our *Eaſtward Indians* were confederate with them.

On the 18th of *Auguſt*, one hundred and forty *French* and *Indians*, in two Sloops, early in the Morning, from *Placentia*, arrived at *Bonoviſt*, and ſurprized the *Pembrook Galley*, the *Society* of *Pool*, and a leſſer Veſſel, in which was thirty Ton of Oil: Capt: *Gill* of *Charleſtown* was there at the ſame time, in a Ship of fourteen Guns, with twenty four Men. He was furiouſly attackt, but defended himſelf with great Courage and good Conduct, from diverſe bold and deſperate Attempts which they made upon him. When he had beat 'em at ſmall Arms, they then brought the Galley to bear upon him with her great Guns, which he return'd in the like Language. They then ſet Fire to the *Society*, with an expectation of burning him alive; but the Wind proving contrary, drove her aſhore on a Rock, where ſhe ſoon conſumed. They then ſet the leſſer Ship on Fire, which burnt to ſuch a degree, by reaſon of the Oil, that it would ſoon have devoured him, had not the Buoy-rope of the Anchor got beteen the Rudder and the Stern, and

kept

kept off the blazing War from him. The scituation of the Fort was such, as that it was not able to protect the Town of St. *Johns*; upon which it was wholly laid in Ashes, the Inhabitants being mostly fled into the Woods. The loss that Capt. *Gill* sustained in the whole Encounter, was but one Man slain and two wounded.

I now return to the *Westward*, where on the 25th of *October*, the Enemy did some Mischief. *Lancaster* was alarm'd, and the Alarm was a means of the untimely Death of the Reverend Mr. *Gardiner*, their worthy Pastor. Several of the Inhabitants, who belonged to the Garrison, were wearied by hard Travelling the Day before, in pursuit of the Enemy. This caused this good Man out of Pity and Compassion, to Watch that Night himself; accordingly he went into the Box, which lay over the Flanker, where he staid till late in the Night: But being cold, (as was supposed) he was coming down to warm himself; when one between Sleeping and Waking, or surpriz'd thro' excess of Fear, fir'd upon him, as he was coming out of the Watch house; where no Man could rationally expect the coming of an Enemy.

Mr. *Gardiner*, altho' he was shot through the Back, came to the Door and bid them open it, for he was wounded. No sooner did he enter, but he fainted away: As he came to himself, he asked who it was that shot him? and when they told him, he pray'd God to forgive him, and forgave him himself, believing that he did it not on purpose; and with a composed frame of Spirit, desired them that bewailed him not to weep, but pray

pray for him, and his Flock. He comforted his sorrowful Spouse, and expired within an hour.

The *Indian* Harvest being now gathered, and the Winter approaching, the Enemy like Beasts of Prey, retired to their private Cells: But concluding it necessary to discover their Head quarters, it was resolved, that Col. *Hilton,* with two hundred and seventy Men, should go to *Naridgwalk* with twenty Days Provision: At which time the Country appeared like a frozen Lake, the Snow four foot deep; yet neither Officers nor Soldiers were in the least discouraged; but when they came unto the Fort, could not discover the least step of an *Indian,* only a few deserted *Wigwams,* and a large Chappel, with a Vestry at the end of it, which they set on fire.

The Winter Season requiring *Snow-shoes,* an Express was sent Col. *Patrick* to supply the Frontiers therewith, which he no sooner forwarded, but the Express was intercepted, by a *Mount-Real* Scout, who robb'd him of *Fifty Pounds* that he had in his Pocket, which at their return they presented to the Governour, who converted it into a *Bowl,* and called it by the Name of the *New-England* Gift.

Early in the Spring, Capt. *Larraby* was ordered to Cruise on the Shore of *L' Accadia,* and defeat the *French* from their Fishery, having *Whale-Boats* to attend him: Capt. *Fowl* was also dispatcht in a Sloop of War, who on the Northward of *Cape-Sables* took a small Vessel formerly belonging to the *English,* which had Cattle and Sheep on Board her. Soon after he took five Prisoners at *Port Rosua,* and three at *L' Have,*
burnt

burnt a few Houses, and kill'd some Cattle; but the Inhabitants were so miserably poor, and their Circumstances so desperate, that they rather chose to be Prisoners among the *English*, than at Liberty among the *French*.

May the 4th. 1705. Capt. *Hill*, who was formerly taken at *Wells*, and carried to *Canada*, was from thence sent by Mounsieur *Vaudriell*, to concert the exchange of Prisoners, who advis'd of one hundred and seventeen that were then with him, and about seventy more with the *Indians*; which unexpected News was very reviving to the dejected Spirits of their mournful Friends; considering the many Deaths they escaped in their Captivity.

Upon the advice hereof, Capt. *Levinston* was sent to *Canada* to capitulate about the matter, and after him Capt. *Appleton*, and Mr. *Sheldon* (with seventy Prisoners of theirs) who went by Water, having ordered a Scout before of ten Men by Land to advise of their coming, that so our Prisoners might be in readiness. But the *Jesuits* and *Fryers* had by this time so influenc'd the Governour, as to cause him to break his Word of Honour, pretending, that as the *Indians* were independant and a free born People, that he had no power to demand any Captives of them; when at the same time they were so much in Subjection, and Vassalage unto him, that they never formed an Enterprize without him, neither did they dare to attempt it without his knowledge.

Now altho' the Expence and Industry of our Commissioners in this Affair was very great; yet notwithstanding they could not obtain above
sixty

sixty Captives out of one hundred and eighty seven; which was scandalously base and dishonourable in that Government.

The descent that the Enemy again made on *New foundland*, was more terrible and surprizing than the former; for on *January* 21st. at break of day, Mounsieur *Supercaſs*, Governour of *Placentia*, came with five hundred and fifty *French* from *Canada, Port-Royal*, and other places adjacent, and a company of Salvages, of whom *Aſſacombuit* was Chief; who ransack'd and laid waste all the *Southern* Settlements in a few Days, and then fell on St. *John*'s, where in the space of two hours all were become Prisoners of War, excepting those in the Castle and Fort. The Night before the Enterprize they were oblig'd to lye on a Bed of Snow, six foot deep, for fear of being discovered, which caused such cold and numbness in the Joynts of several, that the General vow'd revenge, and accordingly Executed his Resentment, for that he destroy'd all before him, and gave no Quarter for some time; till Mounsieur *Boocore*, who was a Gentleman of more Humanity, did interpose and abate his Fury: The Number that they took alive was one hundred and forty, whom they sent unto the Garrison, not out of pity to the Prisoners, but with a design to Starve the whole. After that they laid close seige to the Garrison, and Fort, which continued thirty Days without relief. (Excepting three who made their Escape to the former and seventeen to the latter) In the Fort were only forty Men under the command of Capt. *Moody*, and twelve in the Castle, under Capt. *Lotham*; who behaved themselves

with

with such bravery, that they slighted all manner of tenders that were made them of Surrendring, with the highest Contempt immaginable.

Upon this the Enemy committed many Barbarities, and sent several threatnings; but they had no Influence either on Officers or Soldiers, for they ply'd their Bombs and Mortarpieces to so good Effect, that they kill'd several, and lost but three in the whole Engagement.

After this they Steer'd to *Consumption-Bay*, having first demolish't all the *English* Settlements in *Trinity* and *Bonivist*, where they burnt their Stages and Boats, and laid a Contribution besides upon the Inhabitants. From thence they went to *Carboneer*, where they met with some repulse, and finding their Provision fall short, they sent a further number unto the Fort, reserving the most skilful and able Fishermen for themselves until the succeeding Spring.

During this time our Frontiers at home were greatly infested. At *Spruce-Creek* in *Kittery* they kill'd five and took as many more; among the Slain was Mrs. *Hoel*, a Gentlewoman of good Extract, and Education; but the greatest Sufferer was *Enoch Hutchins* in the loss of his Wife and Children. Three weeks after *John Rogers* was dangerously wounded, and at a little distance *James Toby* was shot by another Party. From thence they went *Westward*, and took a Shallop which belong'd to *Piscataqua*. Our Sea coast at the same time was disrested by *Privateers*, particularly by Capt. *Crepoa*, who notwithstanding our Cruisers that were then out, took seven Vessels, besides a Sloop, and carried them all to *Port-Royal*,

Royal, excepting the latter, which was retaken by Capt. *Harris* at *Richmond*'s Ifland.

About the fame time *Michael Royal*, a Fifherman belonging to *Marblehead*, as he went afhore for wood off of Cape *Sables*, was Barbaroufly cut in peices.; On the 15th. of *October* followlng, eighteen *Indians* fell on Cape *Neddick*, where they took four Children of Mr. *Stovers* at a little diftance from the Garrifon. The youngeft not able to travel was knock't on the head, the other three were carried Captive; but being attack't by Lieut. *March*, and loofing one of their Company, they kill'd a fecond Child in way of revenge.

During the Winter little or no Spoil was done on any of our Frontiers; the Enemy being fo terrified by reafon of *Snow-fhoes* (which moft of our Men were fkilful in) that they never attempted coming at fuch a feafon after.

But as the Spring came on, *April* 27th. 1706. a fmall Body fell on an Out-houfe in *Oyfter-River*, where they kill'd eight, and wounded two; The Garrifon which ftood near, had not a Man in it, at that time; but the Women, who affum'd an *Amazonian* Courage feeing nothing but Death before them, advanc'd the Watch-box, and made an Alarm. They put on Hatts, with their Hair hanging down, and fired fo brifkly that they ftruck a terror in the Enemy, and they withdrew, without firing the houfe, or carrying away much Plunder. The principal Sufferer at this time was *John Wheeler*, who thinking them to be friend *Indians*, unhappily fell under their Fury. Two days after Mr. *Shapleigh* and his Son, as they were

travel-

travelling thro' *Kittery*, were ambusht by another Party, who killing the Father, took the Son, and carried him to *Canada*. In their March they were so inhumanely Cruel, that they *bit* off the tops of his Fingers, and to stagnate the Blood, sear'd them with hot Tobacco Pipes.

June the 1st Mr. *Walker*, being loaden with Provisions from *Connecticut*, was chased by a *French* Privateer, which to avoid he ran ashore in his Boat, and as he hastned to *Road-Island*, made an Alarm all round: The Government there was so expeditious, that in a few Hours (by beat of Drum) one hundred Men well equip'd voluntarily entred on board of two Sloops, under the command of Major *Wanton* and Captain *Paine*, who next Day became Masters of the Prize, wherein were thirty seven Men, under the command of Capt. *Ferrel*, bound for *Port-Royal*, but in his way was obliged to cruise on the *New-England* Coast.

The Year after they did another brave Exploit, in taking a Sloop from *Placentia*, with four Guns, four Patteraroes, and forty nine Men, which undoubtedly prevented great Mischief that otherwise would have befallen us.

Upon the Advice of many *English* Captives that were now at *Port-Royal*, Captain *Rouse* of *Charlestown* was sent with a *Flag of Truce*; who after an unusual stay, returned but with seventeen, saying, that the *French* detained them. He fell under a severe suspicion of carrying on a secret Trade with the Enemy; which grew upon his second going, when he brought but seven back with him.

The *General Assembly* which was then sitting, with the Country throughout, were thrown hereby, into a great Ferment; considering the vast Charge and Effusion of Blood. He was Indicted for Trayterous Correspondence with the Enemy. Others at the same time, like Snakes in the Grass, or Moles under Ground, were as industrious to evade it, and to put a different Gloss on all his Actions.

–––––– *Quid non Mortalia pectora Cogis Auri Sacra fames?* ––––––

And yet it has been generally remark'd from the beginning of Time here, that those who have been *Indian-Traders*, and seemingly got much, have sensibly decay'd, and many of them become Victims to their bloody Cruelty. A *Proclamation* was issued forth to apprehend all such as were Suspected; Several hereupon were seized, and others vehemently Suspected, who did what they could to extenuate the Crime, and to get the Indictment alter'd from that of *Treason*, unto High *Misdemeanour*. At last a Court of *Oyer and Terminer* was call'd, and Fines were imposed, besides the Prison Fees.

How far these unhappy Measures tended to increase our Troubles, is Obvious to an impartial Eye, if we consider how they supply'd the Enemy with Powder, Shot, Iron, Nails, and other Materials of War.

The Advice of Collonel *Schuyler* from time to time was of eminent Service unto the Country, who advis'd of two hundred and seventy Men that were coming upon us. Their first descent was on *Dunstable*, the third of *July*, where they fell on a Garrison that had twenty Troopers posted in it, who by their Negligence and Folly, keeping no Watch suffered them to enter, which tended to the destruction of one half of their Number. After that a small Party attack't *Daniel Galeucias* House, who held them play for some time, till the old Mans Courage fail'd; when on surrendring himself, he inform'd them of the state of the Garrison; how that one Man was kill'd & only two Men and a Boy left; which caused them to rally a new, and with greater Courage than before. Upon which one with the Boy got out on the back side, leaving only *Jacob* to fight the Battle, who for some time defended himself with much bravery; but over power'd with Force, and finding none to assist him, was oblig'd to quit it, and make his escape as well as he could; but before he got far, the Enemy laid hold of him once and again, and yet by much strugling he rescused himself: Upon this they burnt the House, and next Day about forty more fell on *Amesbury*, where they kill'd eight; two, at the same time, who were at work in a Field, hearing an Out-cry, hastned to their Relief; but being pursued, ran to a deserted House, in which were two Flankers, where each of them found an old Gun, but neither of them fit for Service: and if they were, had neither Powder nor Shot to load with: However, each took a Flanker, and made the best appearance they could, by thrusting the Muzzles of their Guns outside the Port-holes, crying aloud, *Here they are, but do not fire till they come nearer*; which put the Enemy into such a fright, that they instantly drew off.

From thence they went to *Kingstown*, where they kill'd and wounded several Cattle. About the same time *Joseph English*, who was a Friend *Indian*, going from *Dunstable* to *Chelmsford*, with a Man and his Wife on Horeback, was shot dead, the Woman taken, but the Man made his escape. On the 8th of *July*, five *Indians* a little before Night, fell on an Out-house in *Reading*, where they surpriz'd a Woman with eight Children; the former with the three youngest were instantly dispatcht, and the other they carried Captive; but one of the Children unable to travel, they knockt on the head, and left in the Swamp, concluding it was dead, but a while after it was found alive. The Neighbourhood being alarm'd, got ready by the Morning, and coming on their Track, pursued them so near, that they recovered three of the Children, and put the Enemy into such a Terrour, that they not only quitted their Plunder and Blankets, but the other Captive also. Several Strokes were afterwards made on *Chelmsford*, *Sudbury* and *Groton*, where three Soldiers as they were going to publick Worship, were way-laid by a small Party, who kill'd two, and made the other a Prisoner.

At *Exeter* a Company of *French Mohauks*, who some time kept lurking about Capt. *Hilton*'s Garrison, took a view of all that went in and out; and observing some to go with their Scythes to mow, lay in ambush till they laid by their Arms, and while at Work, rushed on at once, and by intercepting them from their Arms, kill'd four, wounded one, and carried three Captive: So that out of ten, two only escaped. A while after,

ter, two of those that were taken, *viz.* Mr. *Edward Hall*, and *Samuel Myals*, made their escape; but the Fatigue and Difficulty that they went thro', (besides the terror and fear they were under of being taken) was almost incredible; for in three weeks together they had nothing to subsist on, excepting a few Lilly roots, and the Rhines of Trees.

Several of our Captives still remaining among the *French* and *Indians*, occasioned Mr. *Sheldon*'s going a second time to *Canada* with a Flag of Truce, who at his return brought forty five, and had a prospect of many more, but was prevented by the *Jesuits*.

As to the Treatment of our Captives with the *French*, it was as different and various as their Tempers and Constitutions: Some were mild and pleasant, while others were morose and sordid; but the *Indians* might as well alter their Complexions as their Constitutions; for scarce a Day past without some act of Cruelty, insomuch that all were under a constant Martyrdom between fear of Life and terror of Death.

It would be an endless task to enumerate the various Sufferings that many groaned under, by long Marching with heavy Burdens, thro' heat and cold; and when ready to faint for want of Food, they were frequently knockt on the head: Teeming Women, in cold Blood, have been ript open; others fastned to Stakes, and burnt alive; and yet the Finger of God did eminently appear in several Instances, of which I shall mention a few. As

First,

First. Of *Rebekah Taylor*, who after her return from Captivity, gave me the following Account. *viz.*

That when she was going to *Canada*, on the back of *Mount Real* River, she was violently insulted by *Sampson* her bloody Master, who without any Provocation was resolved to hang her; and for want of a Rope, made use of his Girdle, which when he had fastned about her Neck, attempted to hoise her up on the limb of a Tree, (that hung in the nature of a *Gibbit*) but in hoising her, the Weight of her Body broke it asunder; which so exasperated the cruel Tyrant, that he made a second attempt, resolving that if he fail'd in that, to knock her on the head: But before he had power to effect it, *Bomaseen* came along, who seeing the Tragedy on foot, prevented the fatal stroke.

A second was a Child of Mrs. *Hannah Parsons*, of *Wells*, whom the *Indians* for want of Food, had determined to Roast alive, but while the fire was kindling, and the Sacrifice preparing, a Company of *French Mohauks* came down the River in a Canoo, with three Dogs, which somewhat revived these hungry Monsters, expecting to make a Feast upon one of them. So soon as they got ashore, the Child was offer'd in Exchange; but despising the offer, they tendred a Gun, which they readily accepted, and by that means the Child was preserved.

A third was of *Samuel Butterfield*, who being sent to *Groton* as a Soldier, was with others attackt, as they were gathering in the Harvest; his bravery was such, that he kill'd one and wounded ano-

another, but being overpower'd by strength, was forc'd to submit; and it hapned that the slain *Indian* was a *Sagamore*, and of great dexterity in War, which caused matter of Lamentation, and enrag'd them to such degree that they vow'd the utmost revenge; Some were for whipping him to Death; others for burning him alive; but differing in their Sentiments, they submitted the Issue to the *Squaw Widow*, concluding she would determine something very dreadful, but when the matter was opened, and the Fact considered, her Spirits were so moderate as to make no other reply, than, " *Fortune L' guare*. Upon which some were uneasy; to whom she answered, *If by killing him, you can bring my Husband to life again, I beg you to study what Death you please; but if not let him be my Servant*; which he accordingly was, during his Captivity, and had favour shewn him.

The State of Affairs still looking with a Melancholly Aspect, it was resolved for a more vigorous Prosecution of the War, to grant the following Encouragement. *viz.*

	l.	
To Regular Forces under pay	10 0 0	⎫
To Volunteers in Service	20 0 0	⎬ *per Scalp.*
To Volunteers without pay	50 0 0	⎭
To any Troop or Company that go for the Relief of any Town or Garrison	30 0 0	

Over and above was granted the benefit of Plunder, & Captives of Women & Children under twelve Years of age, which at first seem'd a great
Encou-

Encouragement, but it did not anfwer what we expected. The Charge of the War was by this time fo great, that every *Indian* we had kill'd or taken, coft the Country at leaft a Thoufand Pounds.

But while they continued in great Bodies, they did not commit the like Spoil and Rapine (in proportion) as they did in fmaller. *Auguft* the 10th. they flew *William Pearl* of *Dover,* and a little after took *Nathanael Tibbits.* But of all the *Indians* that was ever known fince King *Phillip,* never any appear'd fo Cruel and Inhumane as *Affacambuit,* that infulting Monfter, who by the Encouragement of the *French* went over to *Paris,* and being introduced to the King, lifted up his Hand in the moft arrogant manner imaginable, faying, *This Hand of mine has Slain one hundred and fifty of your Majefty's Enemies, within the Territorys of New-England* &c. Which bold and impudent Speech was fo pleafing to that Bloody Monarch, that he forthwith Knighted him, & order'd eight Livers a day to be paid him during Life; which fo exalted the Wretch (having his Hands fo long imbrued in innocent Blood) as at his return, to exert a Sovereignty over the reft of his Brethren, by Murthering one, and Stabing another, which fo exafperated thofe of their Relations, that they fought Revenge, and would inftantly have Executed it, but that he fled his Country, and never return'd after.

January 21ft. Collonel *Hilton* with two hundred and twenty Men, vifited the Frontiers anew; but the mildnefs of the Winter prevented his going fo far as he expected; However in his return,

return, near *Black Point*, he came on an *Indian* track which he purfued, and kill'd four; at the fame Time he took a *Squaw* alive with a *Papoofe* at her breft, which he preferved, and fhe was of fingular fervice in conducting him to a Body of eighteen, who lodg'd on a neck of Land; About break of day he Surpriz'd them as they lay afleep, and flew all but one, whom they kept a Prifoner; But it's ftrange to think by what winged Mercury reports are often carried. *Plutarch* I remember, and other Writers, have given furprizing Inftances of things tranfacted at fuch a diftance, as have been inconfiftant with any humane Conveyance. Witnefs that of *Domitian*, two thoufand five hundred Miles in the fpace of twenty four Hours; And of *William* the Conquerour, the news of whofe Death was conveyed from *Roan* to *Rome* the day he dyed, which as Hiftorians mention, was —— prius pene quam nunciari poffit. And to my certain knowledge, on the very Morning that Collonel *Hilton* did this Exploit, it was publickly talkt of at *Portfmouth* in every Article, and with little or no Variation, altho' ninety Miles diftance.

But all this while we were only cutting off the Branches; the *French* in *Canada*, and *Nova Scotia*, who fupply the *Indians* with all neceffarys for the War, were the Root of all our Woe.

Wherefore it was refolved to make an Enterprize on *Nova Scotia*, under the Command of Collonel *March* with two Regiments. *viz.*

G   Col-

Col. *Wainright* ⎫
Lt. Col. *Appleton* ⎬ of the Red
Major *Walton* ⎪
Commanders ⎭

Col. *Hilton* ⎫
Lt. Col. *Wanton* ⎬ of the Blew
Major *Spencer* ⎪
Commanders ⎭

In three Transport Ships, five Briganteens, and fifteen Sloops, with Whaleboats answerable, having her Majestty's Ship the *Debtford*, and the *Province Gally* to cover them.

March 13th. 1707 they sail'd from *Nantasket*, and in a fortnight after, arrived at *Port Royal* Gut, where they landed on both sides the River, which the Enemy observing, made an alarm and retired to the Fort, with what Substance they could get.

Monsieur *Supercass*, who was the Governour, upon rallying his Forces together, held a short Skirmish but finding too warm a Reception, (his Horse being shot under him) was obliged to retreat. A Council of War being called, it was resolv'd that the Artillery should be landed, and their Lines forced: But thro' the Unfaithfulness of some, and cowardly Pretentions of others, little was done in annoying the Enemy, save killing their Cattle, burning their Mills and Out-houses: Whereas if the Officers on board her Majesty's Ship had been true and faithful, matters had succeeded to good advantage. But instead of pressing on, they did rather clog and hinder the Affair: For by crafty Insinuations they afterwards obtained a second Council, which the General not so well weighing as he ought, proved the overthrow of the whole Design. They voted to return; whereas if they had only kept their

Ground,

Ground, and not fired a Gun, the Enemy muft of neceffity have furrendred or have ftarved. This was fo furprifing, that the whole Country was under an amazing Ferment, and the Commander fo grofly reflected on, that his Spirits funk, and he became of little Service ever after: Yet to give him his Character, he was a Man of good Courage, and a true lover of his Country. But the Bufinefs that he undertook, was too weighty for his Shoulders to bear. So foon as his *Excellency* was apprized hereof, (who had the Honour and Intereft of his Country much at Heart) he fent ftrict Orders to ftay them; and another Ship of War, with two Companies of frefh Men to reinforce them; Col. *Hutchinfon*, Col. *Townfend*, and Mr. *Leverett* were appointed Commiffioners, to give the greater Vigour: But the number of Deferters, and difaffected Officers overthrew the whole Affair. However a fecond Attempt was made, which the Enemy perceiving, called in their Auxiliaries both of *French* and *Indians* from *Menis, Sachenecto*, and all other places adjacent. A Privateer and fome other Veffels had alfo arrived fince the withdraw of our Forces. By their Affiftance the Enemy had not only ftrengthned the Fort, but fecured their Lines; fo that nothing could be well attempted but by a few Encounters; in which Major *Walton* behaved himfelf with much Bravery, being the only Field-Officer then afhore; who engaged them fome time, and at laft put them to flight, killing and wounding feveral, among whom was the Field-Major. Thofe that fell on our fide were fixteen, and as many more wounded. Our Frontiers at home were as much difrested as ever : *May* 22d they took two at *Oyster-River*, and on *June* 12th kill'd one at *Groton*; After that they flew *William Carpenter* of *Kittery*, with his whole Family. *July* 8th they way laid a Cart with two Men, as they were going from *Dover* to *Oyster-River*, whom they shot dead. Capt. *Sumersby*, who was there with his Troop, regained the most of the Plunder that they took. About the same time *Stephen Gilman* and *Jacob* his Brother, as they were riding from *Exeter* to *Kingstown*, were ambush'd by another Party. The first had his Horse shot under him, and was in danger of being scalpt before he could get clear: The other Brother had several Shot thro' his Cloaths, and one that graz'd his Belly; his Horse also was wounded; yet he defended himself on Foot, and got into the Garrison.

At *Casco* the *Indians* intercepted a Fishing-boat as she was sailing between the Islands, in which were five Men, three of whom they kill'd, and took the other two. *August* the 10th they waylaid the Road between *York* and *Wells*, and as four Horsemen were riding in Company with Mrs. *Littlefield*, who had the value of *Sixty Pound's* with her, were all slain except one, who made his escape. Another Company falling on *Marlborough*, encompassed two as they were at work in the Field; one of which got clear, and the Neighbourhood meeting together, engaged them so smartly, that the Enemy gave way, leaving twenty four Packs behind; which so exasperated their Spirits, with the loss they sustained, that they slew the Captive which they had taken. On
our

our side two were slain, and two wounded.

At *Exeter* one was kill'd near the Meeting-house; and two days after another at *Kingstown*, but the most afflicting stroke that befell us this season was at *Oyster River*, where thirty *French Mohauks*, who appeared like so many Furys with their naked Bodys painted like Blood, and observing some at work in hewing of Timber, and others driving the Team, they violently fell upon them with such hideous Noise and Yelling, as made the very Woods to eccho. At the first shot they kill'd seven and mortally wounded another, upon which Capt. *Chesly* (who had signally behaved himself in many Encounters) with the few that were left, fired on them with great vigour and resolution; aud for some time gave a check to their Triumphing; but the Enemy being too powerful, soon overcame him, to the great lamentation of all that knew him.

It being now the height of *Indian* Harvest, they disperst themselves, into all parts, and did considerable Mischief; but having somthing more then ordinary in view, they beset *Winter-Harbour*, and on *September* 21*st*. with one hundred and fifty Men in fifty Canoos, Attempted the taking two Shallops as they lay at Anchor, in which were Capt. *Austin*, Mr. *Harmon*, Sergeant *Cole*, and five Men more, with a Boy; who perceiving their Intention, suffer'd them to paddle till they had got near, and then fired, which put them into great Confusion. But they soon recover'd themselves & fir'd on our Men with such resolution, as made them to quit one of their Boats, by cutting their roads and lashings; and no sooner had they taken

pos-

possession thereof, but they got their Mainsail atrip, before that our Men could get up theirs half Mast high, and then put out their Oars, which they joyn'd with Paddles on each side; but having no fargood, and their Boat a dull sailor, ours gain'd on them so much, that they got twelve or thirteen Canoos a head, with Fishing-lines to tow them. But a breeze springing up, & the Enemy making too near the Wind, (for want of a fargood) came to stays several times, in so much that they fell a quarter of a Mile a stern. But the rest of the Canoos kept on firing, and our Men on them for a considerable time together. The only Man we lost was *Benjamin Daniel*, who was shot thro' the Bowels soon after they came to sail; At his fall he said, " *I am a dead Man!* yet recovering himself a little added, " *Let me kill one before I dye!* but he had not strength to fire.

The Engagement held about three hours, in which the *English* spent five pounds of Powder, & when the Enemy ceased their chase, they had not above one quarter of a pound left. The *Indians* were so bold and daring, as to attempt to take hold of the blades of their Oars, as they were rowing. The number of them that fell was then unknown, because of a continued Cloud of Smoke; but it was affirmed, that nine were Slain, and twice as many wounded. ——— After this a small Scout appear'd at *Barwick*, where they kill'd two as they return'd from worship; Upon which some of the Inhabitants who were acquainted with their walk, lay in wait, and making the first discovery fired to good advantage; which put

put them into so great a Consternation, that they dropt their Packs, in which were three Scalps, supposed to be some of those which a little before were taken at *Oyster River*. The Winter Season afforded a little respite: But on *April* 22. 1708. Lieut. *Littlefield* of *Wells*, with *Joseph Winn*, as they were travelling to *York*, were surrounded by a small Body; the latter made his escape, but the other was carried to *Quebeck*, who being a skilful *Engineer*, especially in Water works, did them great Service.

About this time eight hundred *French* and *Indians* were forming a desperate design against us, but on a division among themselves fell short of the Mischief they designed us. However one hundred and fifty on *August* 29th at break of day, fell on *Haverhill*, and passing by the Garrisons got into the very Center of the Town before they were discovered. They attempted to fire the Meeting-house, and after that did burn several Houses near it. Major *Turner*, Capt. *Price*, & Capt. *Gardner*, were happily there at that time, and rallied together what Forces they could; but most of their Men being posted in remote Garrisons, were unable to assist them However with such as they could get together, they faced the Enemy with much bravery, and in less than an hour put them all to flight, leaving nine of their dead, and carrying off several that were wounded. But the Slain on our side were thrice as many, by reason of the surprize that they at first were in; among whom was the Reverend Mr. *Rolph* the worthy Minister of that Town, with Capt. *Wainright*.

(48)

A while after *James Hays* of *Amesbury* was taken, and one at *Brookfield*; they also kill'd *Robert Reed* and *David Hutchins* of *Kittery*.

Collonel *Hilton* again march'd toward their Head quarters with one hundred and seventy Men at *Amassaconty*, *Pigwacket*, and other places adjacent; but after a long and tedious March could make no discovery.

On *April* 12th. 1709. a Scout fell on *Deerfield*, and took *Mehamen Hinsdel*, as he was driving a Cart, which was the second time of his Captivity. And on *May* 6th. another Party within three Miles of *Exeter*, surpriz'd several as they were going to a Saw-mill, among whom were Mr. *William Moody*, *Samuel Stephins*, and two of Mr. *Jeremiah Gilman*'s Sons, whom they carried Captive. A few Days after Capt. *Wright* of *Northampton*, with several *English*, and two *Natick Indians*, adventuring to the Lake, within forty miles of Fort *La' Motte*, kill'd and wounded two or three of the *French Mahauks*; and on their return up *French*-River, met with another Body of the Enemy in Canoos, on whom they fir'd, and overset, kill'd and wounded several of them. In this Company was *William Moody* before mentioned, who being now alone with but one *Indian* in a Canoo, was encouraged by the *English* to kill said *Indian*, and make his escape. Which he attempted, but overset the Canoo in the struggle, and then *Moody* swam towards the *English* for Relief. Whereupon Lieut. *John Wells*, with one or two more, ran down the Bank and helpt him ashore. In the mean time a number of the Enemy came to the Bank, and wounded *John Strong*, and

and kill'd the *Lieutenant*, who had been a Man of very good Courage, and well spirited to serve his Country, and so the loss of him was much lamented. Hereupon *Moody* unhappily resign'd himself again into the Enemies hands; who most innumanly tortured him, by fastning him unto a Stake, and roasting him alive; whose Flesh they afterwards devoured. Our Men considering they were so far in the *Indians* Country, and like to be encompass'd, were forc'd to make a running Fight. So scattering in the Woods, lost *John Burt* who was supposed to perish with hunger.

The Town of *Deerfield*, which had suffer'd so much Spoil before by Monsieur *Artell*, was on *June* 23d oblig'd to a new Encounter, by Monsieur *Ravell* his Son-in-Law, who with one hundred and eighty *French* and *Indians*, expected to lay all desolate: But the Town being alarm'd, they valiantly resisted, with the loss only of one Man, and another wounded. After that the Enemy kill'd two at *Brookfield*, one at *Wells*, and took another Captive.

Col. *Vetch* who was now in *England*, and well acquainted with the Continent of *America*, was very sensible that the reduction of *Canada* was of absolute necessity, for subduing the *Indians*; upon which he laid a Plan of the whole Country before some of the chief Ministers of State, representing every thing in its true Light. General *Nicholson* added all his Interest to the Motion made by Col. *Vetch*, and between them they obtain'd a promise for sufficient Forces both by Sea and Land, for the Conquest of *Canada*. They arrived early in the Spring, with her *Majesty's*

H   Royal

Royal Commands and Instructions to the *Governours* of the several *Provinces,* to furnish their respective Quota's. To such as should offer volunteers, they presented a good Firelock, Cartouchbox, Flints, Ammunition, a Coat, Hat and Shirt; with an assurance of her *Majesty*'s Princely Favour unto all such as should distinguish themselves.

Upon this the several *Governours* contributed their utmost Assistance; and considering that *New-York* (with the adjacent places) lay nearest the *Lake,* it was resolved that Col. *Nicholson* should command the several Troops from thence, for the attacking of *Mount-Real,* while Col. *Vetch* was preparing to head the Forces by Sea.

But it often happens in the course of Divine Providence, that when our Expectations are at the highest, things come to nothing. For while our Forces were ready, and after a vast Expence by long waiting, there was a stop at home from any further proceeding for that time; which occasioned Col. *Nicholson* to imbarque again for *England,* to revive the Expedition, if possible. But such was the importance of Affairs then on foot, that notwithstanding his indefatigable Care and Pains, he could not effect it. However he obtained a sufficient Force for the reduction of *Port-Royal* and *Nova Scotia,* which was so prejudicial to our Fishery and Merchandize.

Its Scituation is from 43 to 51 degrees of *North Lanitude,* and is part of the *Terra Canadensis,* whose Bounds are, the Atlantick Ocean on the North, *Briton* Island and the Bay of Saint *Laurence* to the *East, Canada* to the *West,* and *New Englaud*

to

to the *South*; whose first seizure was by Sir *Sebastian Cobbet* for the Crown of *Great Britain*, in the Reign of King *Henry the seventh*; but lay dormant till the Year 1621. In which time, Sr. *William Alexander*, who was then one of the Secretaries of State for *Scotland*, and afterwards Earl of Sterling, had a Patent for it from *King James*, where he settled a Colony and possess't it some Years. After that Sr. *David Kirk* was Proprietor as well as Governour, but did not enjoy it long; for to the surprize of all thinking Men, it was given up unto the *French*; but *Oliver* who had a forseeing Eye of the danger that would ensue unto the *British* Interest, from its being in the hands of so potent an Enemy, retook it in the Year 1654. and in no after Treaties would be perswaded to surrender it: Yet in 1662. it was again given up, unto the Shame and Scandal of the *English*.

Monsieur *Maneval* was then made Governour, who built a small Fort at *Port Royal*, which lies on the edge of a Basin one League broad, and two long, about sixteen foot of Water on one side, and six or seven on the other, where the Inhabitants drove a considerable Trade, and increased much in the adjacent Parts, till Sr. *William Phips* in the Year 1690, took possession of it in the Name of King *William* and Queen *Mary*, and administred the Oaths of Allegiance to the Inhabitants; but in a little time they revolted. Col. *Nicholson* arrived at *Boston July* the first, 1710. in her Majesty's Ship *Dragon*, attended by the *Falmoth* and a *Bombship*, with several Transports, *British* Officers, a Regiment of *Marines*, Provisions and Stores of War; bringing with him her

Majesty's Royal Command to the several *Governours* of the *Massachusetts, Newhampshire, Connecticut* and *Rhode-Island,* to be assisting in the said Expedition; who very readily obeyed, and supply'd their respective Quota's of good effective Men, with Transports, Provision. Stores of War, *Pilots, Chaplains, Chirurgeons,* and all Necessaries for the Service.

Col. *Nicholson* was appointed *General and Commander in chief,* who Embarqued *September* 18th. from *Nantasket* having with him ———

Her Majestys Ship the *Dragon,* Commadore *Martyn,*
  The *Falmouth* ——— Capt. *Riddle*
  The *Lowstaff* ——— Capt. *Gordon*
  The *Feversham* ——— Capt. *Pastor*
  The *Province Galley* —— Capt. *Southack*
  The *Star Bomb* ——— Capt. *Rochfort.*

Besides *Tenders, Transports, Hospiptals, Store-ships,* and twenty five lesser Vessels, with open Floats for carrying Boards and necessaries for the Cannon. The *Land-Forces* consisted of *five Regiments* of Foot, whereof Col. *Vetch* was *Adjutant General,* Sir *Charles Hobby,* Col. *Walton,* Col. *Tailer,* Col. *Whiting,* and Col. *Reading,* had Commissions sent them from the *Queen.* The Wind proving fair, they all safe arrived in six Days, excepting Capt. *Taye,* who at his entring into the Gut was lost with twenty five Men. Next Day a Council of War was held, and several Detachments ordered to go ashore, and view the Ground for the better landing and pitching their Camp. Col. *Reading*
           and

and Col. *Rednap*, with a Company of *Marines*, were appointed on the *South* side of the River where the Fort stood, and supported with one hundred and fifty Men more under the command of Major *Mullins* : At the same time Col. *Vetch*, Col *Walton*, Major *Brown*, Capt. *Southack*, and Engineer *Forbes*, landed on the *North* side with a Company of *Granadeers*, commanded by Capt. *Mascareen*. After this Orders were given to land the whole Army, which was done by four a Clock in the Afternoon. The Fort fired on them, but did no Damage. In the Evening the *Bomb-Ship* came up, and saluted them with seven *Shels*, which number the Fort returned, but without Execution. On *Thursday* the twenty sixth at break of Day, the *General* march'd with the Army on the *South* side, the *Marines* in the Front, Col. *Reading* at their head, Col. *Whiting*'s Regiment in the Center, Sir *Charles Hobby* in the Reer, and Major *Levingston* with a Party of *Indians* flanking the Body in their March. Towards Evening the Fort fired very smartly, and so did the *French* and *Indians* with their small Arms, as they lay behind the Fences, who kill'd three of our Men. Upon landing the Stores, which were brought up in the Night, the Enemy discharged several times from the Fort. Next Day we mounted some of our Guns, and made preparations to bring up the flat bottom Boats with the Artillery and Ammunition. In the Evening our *Bomb-Ship* came up again, and threw thirty six Shells into the Fort, which put them into such an amazing Terror, as brought to my Mind the saying of the Poet,

The

*—The slaughter-breathing Brass grew hot and spoke,
In flames of Lightning, and in clouds of Smoke.*

After that Lieut. Col. *Ballantine* with his Company from the Fleet, and Lieut. Col. *Goff* from Col. *Vetch* on the *North*, with four Companies more, came to the *General's Camp*: Every Regiment was now preparing for further Engagements, the Cannon being all landed; Lieut. Col. *Johnson* with three hundred was ordred to cut *Fascines*, the Boats being constantly employed in going and coming with Provisions and all sorts of Warlike Stores. On *Friday* the twenty ninth two *French* Officers, a *Fort Major Sergeant* and *Drummer*, came out of the Fort with a Flag of Truce, and a Letter from Monsieur *Supercass*, unto the *General*, respecting some Gentlewomen that were terrified at the Noise of *Bombs*, praying his Protection, and that no Incivility or Abuse might be done them, which was granted. Next Day the Centinels of our advanced Guards discovered some of the Enemy near the Woods, whom they pursued, and took Capt. *Allein* a Prisoner. *October* 1st. the great Guns were plac'd on three Batteries; the *Mortars* were also planted, and twenty four *Cohorns* at a little distance from the outward Barrier of the Fort. These all play'd upon the Fort with good Effect; the *French* at the same time firing their great Guns and Mortars upon us. The General sent Col. *Tailer* and Capt. *Abbercromy* with a Summons to Monsieur *Supercass* the Governour, to deliver up the Fort for the *Queen of Great Britain*, as her undoubted
Right.

Right. The Answer which he return'd was soft, only *desiring a Capitulation with some of the principal Officers on each side,* which was granted; and thereupon a Cessation of Arms. Next Day the Articles of *Capitulation* were drawn up and signed by General *Nicholson* and the *Governour.* Upon this several Compliments pass'd on each side, which were sent by Major *Handy* the *Aid-de-Camp*: And on *October* 5th the Fort was delivered up. Upon which Major *Abbercromby,* with two hundred Men, five *Captains,* and eight *Subalterns,* were ordered to take possession thereof. Capt. *Davison* marched first at the head of fifty Granadeers; Major *Abbercromby,* Capt. *Mascareen,* Capt. *Bartlett,* Capt. *Adams,* and Capt. *Lyon,* followed in their proper Stations; the *General,* with Col. *Vetch* on his right Hand, and Sir *Charles Hobby* on the left; with Monsieur *Bonaventure* and *D'Gouten* who were Hostages; and then the *Field-Officers,* with a great many others advanced to the Fort; where the *French* Governour met them half way on the Bridge, with Col. *Reading* and Capt. *Matthews,* who were Hostages on our side, and complimented him in these Words.

Sir, *I am very sorry for the King my Master, in loosing so brave a Fort, and the Territories adjoyning; but count my self happy in falling into the Hands of one so Noble and Generous, and now deliver up the Keys of the Fort, and all the* Magazine *into your Hands, hoping to give you a Visit next Spring.* Which Keys the *General* immediately delivered to Col. *Vetch,* as Governour of the Fort, by vertue of her Majesty's Instructions: Whereupon Monsieur *Supercass* with his Officers and Troops marched out
with

with Drums beating, Colours flying, and Guns shouldered; each paying their Respects to the *General* as they passed by; and then our Army entred the Fort, hoisted the *Union-Flag,* and drank the *Queen*'s Health firing all the Guns round the Fort; as likewise did the Men of War, and other Vessels in the River.

On the Success of these her Majesty's Arms, a Day of Thanksgiving was solemniz'd; and agreeable to the Articles of Capitulation, three Vessels were appointed to transport the Soldiers unto *France,,* being two hundred and fifty eight; who besides the common Allowance, had a considerable stock of Wine, Brandy, Sugar, Spice, and other things, with a plentiful supply for the late Governour. After this a Council of War was call'd, who resolved, that Major *Levinston*, with St. *Casteen*, and three *Indian* Guides, should go to the Governour of *Canada*, about the Exchange of Captives, and inform him how Matters were here. Their first arrival was at *Penobscot*, at St. *Casteen*'s House, who courteously entertained him. From thence they went to the Island of *Lett,* where they met with fifty Canoos and twice as many Indians, besides Women and Children; where were two *English* Prisoners, taken a little before at *Winter-Harbour.* Two Days after one of the Prisoners made his escape from an Island where he was hunting with his Master, carrying with him both his Canoo and Gun, and left him behind; which so exasperated the Wretch, that when he got from thence, and came where Major *Levinston* was, he took him by the Throat with

his

his Hatchet in his Hand, ready to give him the fatal ſtroke, had not St. *Caſteen* interpoſed; He was however kept Priſoner ſome time; but by the prudent management and mediation of that Gentleman was releaſed. *November* the 4th. they took their departure, and next day the Majors *Canoo* overſate, drowning one *Indian*, where he alſo loſt his Gun and all he had; after that coming among the Ice, their Canoo was cut to pieces, which obliged them to travel the reſt of the way by Land, thro' horrible Deſerts and Mountains, being often forced to head Rivers and Lakes, and ſome times Knee deep in Snow; ſcarce paſſing a day without fording ſome River or other, which in ſome places were very rapid and dangerous; & for nineteen days together never ſaw the Sun, the Weather being very ſtormy and full of Fogs, and the Trees ſo prodigious thick, that in many places it was with difficulty they got thro': being moſtly Spruce, and Cedar, and the way under foot ſo extream rocky, that it was almoſt next to an impoſſibility. At laſt their Proviſions were wholly ſpent, ſo that for ſix days together they had not one morſel to eat but what they ſcraped off the frozen Earth, or off the bark of Trees. After theſe unſpeakable Difficulties they arrived at *Quebeck December* the ſixteenth, where they were handſomely entertained, and after ſome time of Refreſhment, diſcours'd about the Priſoners. The *Governour* at their return, ſent two Gentlemen with them to *Boſton*, to treat on the ſame head. Six Days homeward his Man fell ſick, whom he left in a Hoſpital at *Troy River*. From thence they came to *Shambiee*, and brought with them

three

three birch Canoos, being thirteen in number; which Canoos they carried seventy Miles by Land, thro' the Woods and Ice, and then passed in them sixty Miles by Water, crossing the Lake. They did not arrive at *Albany* till *February* 23d.

Early in the Spring the Enemy appeared as insulting as ever: The first that fell under their Cruelty was *Benjamin Prebble* of *York*; but the most affecting and surprizing Stroke was on Col. *Hilton* of *Exeter*, who being deeply engaged in the Masting Affair, and having several Trees of value that were fell'd fourteen miles up the Country, went out with seventeen Men to peel off the Bark for fear of Worms: But not being so careful and watchful as they ought to be, on *July* the twenty second they were ambush'd by a Body of *Indians* that were making a descent upon us. They took two and kill'd three, whereof the Collonel was one; which so surpriz'd the rest, (their Guns being wet) that they all ran without firing one shot, or making the least Reprisal. This caus'd the Enemy to triumph, and the more because they slew a superiour Officer, whom they soon scalpt, and with utmost revenge struck their Hatchets in his Brains, leaving a Lance at his Heart. Next day about a hundred Men went in pursuit of them, but could not discover any. One of the slain was buried on the spot, the other two brought home, where the Collonel was decently interr'd, the several Troops in great Solemnity attending his Corps. He was a Gentleman of good Temper, Courage and Conduct, respected and lamented by all that knew him.

After

After this the Enemy appear'd very bold and insolent in the Town, in open Streets; where they carried Captive four Children as they were at play. They then took *John Wedgwood*, whom they carried to *Canada*, and after that kill'd *John Magoon*, of whom one thing is remarkable; that three Nights before he dreamt he should be slain by the *Indians*, at a certain place near his Brother's Barn; which place he frequently visited with a melancholly Countenance, telling several of the Neighbourhood, that within a little while he should be kill'd, and pointed to the very spot, which fell out accordingly.

After this they bent their fury *Westward*, where at *Water-bury* they kill'd three, and one at *Simsbury*. About the same time they fell on *Brookfield*, and then at *Marlborough*, where they shot the *Post* as he was riding to *Hadly*. From thence they went to *Chelmsford*, where they wounded Major *Tyng*, who soon after expired; he was a true lover of his Country, and had very often distinguish'd himself a Gentleman of good Valour and Conduct.

August the 2d. between forty and fifty *French* & *Indians* fell on *Winter-Harbour*, where they kill'd a Woman and took two Men, one whereof was Mr. *Pendleton Fletcher*, which was the fourth time of his Captivity; but he was soon redeem'd by the Garrison. The week after they came with a far superiour Number, kill'd three, and carryed away six, one of the slain they barbarously Skin'd, and made themselves Girdles of his Skin. The last that fell this Season was *Jacob Garland* of *Cochecho*, in his returning from publick Worship.

As the Winter approached, Collonel *Walton* was again preparing to traverse the *Eastern* Shore with an hundred and seventy Men, being the usual Season of visiting their Clam-banks, where one of the Enemy very happily fell into his Hands as they were encamping on an Island; for by the smoak that the *English* made, they came near, concluding them to be some of their own Tribe, but finding themselves deceived, they attempted to escape, which our Men prevented. The Principal *Indian* among them was *Arruhawikwahemt*, chief Sachem of *Naridgwalk*, an active bold Fellow, and one of an undaunted Spirit; for when they ask't several Questions he made them no Reply, and when they threatned him with Death, he laught at it with contempt; upon which they delivered him up unto our friend *Indians*, who soon became his Executioners; but when the *Squaw* saw the destiny of her Husband, she became more flexible, and freely discovered where each of them encampt. Upon this they went further *East*, and took three more; after that a certain *Indian* (thro' discontent) surrender'd himself, and informed of *Mauxus* and several others that were at *Penobscot*, which our Forces had regard unto; and as they returned went up *Saco* River, where they took two, and kill'd five more. Now altho' the Number that we destroyed of them seems inconsiderable to what they did of ours, yet by Cold, Hunger, and Sickness, at least a third of them was wasted since the War begun. For as their number at first (among the several Tribes) were computed *four hundred* and *fifty* fighting Men from *Penobscot*, *Westward*, they were

now

now reduc'd to about *three hundred*, which made the Old Men weary of the War, and to covet Peace. At *Winter-Harbour* they took Corporal *Ayers*, but soon releas'd him, without offering him the least Injury, and then went unto the Fort with a Flag of Truce professing their desire of a Pacification. Yet in a few Days after some came in an Hostile manner at *Cochecho*, where they slew *Thomas Downs* and three more while at Work in the Field. After that, they went to *York*, where they kill'd one and wounded another, who afterwards got to the Garrison and reported, that as they were fishing in the Pond they were way-laid by five *Indians*, one of which ran furiously at him, and knockt him on the head; after this they Scalp'd him, and cut him deep in the Neck. He perfectly retained his Senses, but made not the least motion or struggle, and by this means sav'd his Life. *April* the twenty ninth the like number appear'd at *Wells*, where they kill'd two Men as they were planting of Corn. After that they slew *John Church* of *Cochecho*,; and then way-laid the People as they return'd from publick Worship; where they wounded one, and laid violent Hands on another, but upon firing their Guns, some who were before, return'd and rescued the Prisoner. Upon this Col. *Walton* went with two Companies of Men to *Ossipe* and *Winnepisseocay* Ponds, being places of general Resort for Fishing, Fowling and Hunting; but saw none, only a few deserted *Wigwams*; for being so closely pursued from one place to another, they removed to other Nations, leaving only a few Cut-throats behind, which kept the Country in a constant Alarm. Col.

Col. *Nicholson* by the Reduction of *Port Royal*, (which from that time bears the Name of *Annapolis Royal*) was but the more inflamed with the desire of the Conquest of *Canada*. Wherefore upon his return to *England*, he so effectually represented to the *Queen* and *Ministry*, the great Advantage that would accrue unto the *Crown* thereby, that he obtained Orders for a sufficient Force both by Sea and Land, with the assistance of the several Colonies. And for the better expediting the same, he set sail the latter end of *April*, some time before the Fleet, with express Orders unto the several Governours of *New-England*, *New-York*, the *Jerseys*, and *Philadelphia*, to get their Quota's of Men in readiness. He arrived at *Boston* on *June* the eighth, 1711. to the great Joy and Satisfaction of the Country. A Congress hereupon was appointed at *New-London*, being nearest the Center, where the several *Governours* met, with a firm Resolution of carrying on the important Affairs. On the 25th the Castle gave a Signal of Ships in the Bay, which prov'd to be the Fleet: Upon which the Troops of Guards, and Regiment of Foot were under Arms to receive them: And as his *Excellency* was not yet return'd, the Gentlemen of the Council and others of Distinction, went to congratulate them.

Brigadier *Hill* was Commander in Chief of these her Majesties Troops, and Sr. *Hovenden Walker* Admiral of the Fleet; which consisted of fifteen Men of War, forty Transports, a Battalion of *Marines* and seven *Regiments* under Collonel *Kirk*, Collonel *Segmore*, Brigadier *Hill*, Collonel *Disnee*,

Difnee, Collonel *Windrefs*, Collonel *Clayton* and Collonel *Kaine*, with upwards of *five thoufand Men*, who arrived fafe in Health, & encamped on *Nodles Ifland*, where the *General* invited the *Governour* to view them under Arms. They made the finest appearance that was ever yet feen or known in *America*. Her *Majefty* out of her Royal Favour was alfo pleafed to fend fix Ships with all manner of Warlike Stores, and a fine Train of *Artillery* with forty Horfes to draw the fame.

It's furprizing to think how vigoroufly this Expedition was forwarded, while at *Bofton*, altho' a Town but of Eighty Years ftanding, out of a howling Wildernefs; yet fcarce any *Town* in the Kingdom (but where Stores are laid up before) could have effected the fame in fo fhort a time. For in lefs than a Month the whole Army was fupply'd with ten weeks Provifion, and all other Neceffaries that were wanted; Befides two Regiments of our *New-England* Forces, under the Command of Collonel *Vetch* and Collonel *Walton*; who embarq'd at the fame time in Tranfports of our own. On the day that the Fleet Sail'd, Collonel *Nicholfon* fet out for *New York*, & from thence for *Albany*, having ordered *Battoes* before, and every thing elfe on the Inland Frontiers, to be in readinefs for paffing the *Lake* with utmoft Application. The Affembly of *New-York* raifed ten thoufand Pounds, befides their Proportion of Men, the *Jerfeys* five, and altho' *Penfilvania* was not fo free of their Perfons becaufe of their Perfwafion, yet were as Generous in their Purfe, as any of the other Colonys in carrying on the Expedition.

Every

Every thing now look'd with a Smiling Aspect of Success considering the powerful Strength by Land and Sea, the former being as fine Regimental Troops as any that belong'd to the Duke of *Marlborough*'s Army; and the latter as Serviceable Ships as any in the whole *Navy*, which for better Satisfaction I have here inserted.

The *Swiftzure* to lead with *Starboard*,
The *Monmouth* with the *Larboard Tack* aboard.

Ships Names.	Captains.	Men.	Guns.
Swiftzure	*Joseph Soans*	444	70
Sunderland	Gore	365	60
Enterprize	Smith	190	40
Saphire	Cockburn	190	40
Windsor	Artiss	365	60
Kingstown	Winder	365	60
Montague	Walton	365	60
Devonshire	Cooper	520	80
Edgar, Sr. *H. Walker* Admiral		470	70
Humber	Colliford	520	80
Dunkirk	Rouse	365	60
Feversham	Paston	196	36
Leopard	Cook	280	50
Chester	Mathews	280	54
Monmouth	Mitchel	440	70
15	15	5351	890

The first Harbour they made after they sail'd from *Nantasket*, was Cape *Gaspey*, from thence they sail'd up St. *Laurence*'s River, until they got up off the *Virgin-Mountains*; the Weather then proving

proving foggy, and the Wind freshning, the *Admiral* ask'd the *Pilots* what was best to do ? who advised that as the Fleet was on the *North* Shore, it would be best to bring too, with their heads unto the *Southward* : but he obstinately refusing, acted the reverse, and ordered their heads unto the *North*, which was so astonishing unto the *Pilots*, that one and another foretold their Fear (unto the Officers) and the Destiny that would attend them before the Morning; which accordingly fell out. For at one of the Clock nine Ships with 1500. Men were all cast ashore, and most of the rest in as eminent danger; but so soon as the former struck, they fired their Guns, which gave Caution to the rest : Some of which wore, and stood off; others were so encompassed by the *Breakers* that they were oblig'd to bring too their Anchors, which was their last Refuge ; but before the day approached, the Wind happily shifted to *W. N. W.* upon which they cut their Cables and came to sail. Soon after a Council of War was call'd, but the result not known until the Evening, and then the *Flag* bore away to *Spanish River*, without giving the usual Signal : On which many of the windward Ships were left behind ; but a small Man of War was ordered to Cruise the next day for those that were left, and to take up such as might be alive among the dead, who were about six hundred. After this they made towards the Fleet, but were eight days in getting down ; during which time the Wind was *Eastwardly*, and had our Fleet proceeded, (as it were to be wish'd they had) might easily have got unto *Quebeck* in forty eight Hours.

K   Upon

Upon this difafter the whole Country (and indeed the Nation) was alarm'd, and many Cenfures and Jeloufies arofe; fome imputing it to Cowardize, but moft to Treachery, and the fecret Influence of fome Malecontents then at Helm; otherwife why would a matter of fuch vaft Importance to the *Britifh* Kingdom, be hufh't up in filence, and the Principal Officers not Summon'd to appear. If the *Admiral* was in fault wherefore was he not call'd to an Account? Or why did not the *General* to vindicate himfelf, lay a Remonftrance before the Council Board? And the *Pilots*, (who were order'd from hence at fo great a Charge to the Country to reprefent matters in a true light) been examined? But inftead thereof, difmift without being ask'd one Queftion. However one thing is remarkable, that among thofe that were fhipwrack'd and loft their lives, there was but one fingle Perfon that belong'd to *New-England* among them.

Collonel *Nicholfon* at this juncture was induftrioufly engaged in getting the *Battoes* ready for paffing the *Lake* with a confiderable Number of Friend *Indians*, as well as Englifh, for the attacking of *Mount Real*, which next to *Quebeck* was the place of greateft Importance in all the *French* Territories. But juft as he was ready to embarque an Exprefs came and gave an Account of the miferable Difafter that befel the Fleet: Whereas, if he had proceeded, his whole Army would probably have been cut off; For upon advice of our Fleets misfortune, the *French* drew off all their Auxiliaries and moft of their *Militia* to reinforce *Mount Real*, being advis'd of the defcent that was

ma-

making on them. So great was our loss in this Enterprize that it Affected the whole Country seven Years after; as the Advance & Expence of so much Money and Provisions might well do. And it as much flusht the Enemy; for out of the ruins of our Vessels they not only got much Plunder, but fortified their Castle and out Batteries with a considerable Number of Cannon. They moreover stirr'd up the *French* and *Indians* about *Annapolis Royal* to revolt from their Allegiance to the Crown. Capt *Pigeon* being ordered up the River for Timber to repair the Fort, was violently attackt by no less than one hundred and fifty, who kill'd the whole Boats Crew, wounded the Fort *Major*, and afterwards very barbarously Murdered him: They also slew Capt. *Forbis* the Engineer, besides several others, and took thirty four of them Prisoners. Soon after this, we were informed of the Arrival of our *British* Forces in *England*, on the 9th. of *October* at *Portsmouth*, where on the 15th following, the Admirals Ship the *Edgar* was accidentally blown up, with 400 Seamen and several other People on board, all the Officers being on shore.

The reduction of *Canada* was a matter of great Consequence, not only to the Interest of *New-England* and the adjacent Colonies; but also to the whole *British* Empire. Not that in it self it is of such intrinsick Value; for that the Cold is so great, and the Ice so rigid, as to imbargo it more than half the Year: But as the ingenious Mr. *Dummer* observes in a Letter of his to a Noble Lord in the Year 1712, the Consequence would be very valuable; for as it extends above one thousand Leagues towards the *Meſſiſippi*, it would require a vaſt conſumption yearly of the *Engliſh* Manufactury to ſupport it; there being ſo great a number of ſeveral Nations that live behind, which bring down vaſt quantities of Furs of all ſorts, as amount to an incredible Sum. But her Majeſty's Royal Aim, as he notes, was not ſo immediately to advance a Trade, as the Security and Peace of her good Subjects in *North America*; being thorowly apprized that ſo long as the *French* inhabit there, ſo long the *Engliſh* would be in hazard.

The *Hudſon's Bay* Company, as well as *New-foundland*, have given a melancholly Account of the many Ravages that have been committed there by the powerful Aſſiſtance of thoſe *Salvages*. I'm not inſenſible that many have blamed *New-England*, and caſt the Odium wholly on them for not ſucceeding in this Enterprize; but why *New-England* ſhould be branded with ſuch Infamy, I never could yet hear the Grounds, or any Reaſon aſſigned, but what ſprung from ſome capricious Brains, who were no well wiſhers either to the Cauſe or Country, and would ſtigmatize us if poſſibe, as Enemies to the *Church*, and Diſloyal to our *Sovereign*. But why Enemies to the *Church*? or wherein is it that we differ from them? ſave only in the *Ceremonies*, which none of them will allow to be Eſſential. We indeed are called *Diſſenters*; but many of thoſe that are of the *Church*, diſſent more from one another than we do: For what we diſſent from, is, (as they themſelves term it) only in matters of Indifferency; but many of them are Diſſenters

ters from their own *Articles of Faith*. Is not our *Doctrine* the same? the *Sabbath* as strictly solemnized? and our Mode of Worship as agreeable to the primitive Constitution, as any other Church in the World? Not but that we have degenerated from the pious Steps of our Fore-fathers; yet I am bold to say, that as to number, there are as many sincere and good People in *New-England*, as in any one part of the World. But I beg pardon for this Digression, which is only to wipe off the Calumny that is too often cast upon us. Now as to our *Loyalty*, such pregnant Instances may be given thereof, as will be surprizing to Posterity. Witness our generous and noble Undertaking in the reduction of *Port Royal* under Sir *William Phips*; and after that in the Year 1690. in our descent on *Canada*, where we lost many hundred brave Men, and at our own Cost expended upwards of *one hundred and forty thousand Pounds* in Money, without any Allowance or Assistance from the Crown. After this a new descent on *Port-Royal*, which altho' we miscarried in that also, yet as Mr *Dummer* observes, we were not dispirited in raising another Body of Troops under the Command of Collonel *Nicholson*. And all this under the oppression of twenty Years War before by the *French*, and *Indians*. Yet in the last fatal Expedition, we supplyed more than our *Quota* which the *Queen* assigned; Besides great Sums were advanced to furnish the *British* Forces, which but few Towns in the Kingdom of *England* were able to effect; and none could do it with greater Alacrity and chearfulness of Spirit then we did.

In

In the History of Sr. *Sebastian Cobbet*, which I before hinted, we were informed that he took the great River of St. *Laurence* for the Crown of *Great Britain* in the Reign of King *Henry* the seventh, which according to the *French* Historians, contains almost 2000 Miles in length and 840 in breadth, Scituate between the 39th and 64th Degrees of *North* Latitude, which takes in *Acadia*, *Newfoundland* and *Terra De Laborador*. This great Territory in the beginning of the last Century, by the Contrivance of some then at Helm, was taken possession off by the *French*, who since that have made many fine Settlements, more especially at *Mount Real* and *Queebeck*. The latter is called a City commanded by a Castle, which stands on an Eminence, in which are five Churches, a Cathedral, a Bishop and 12 Prebendaries. Our unhappy Disappointment against *Canada* gave great uneasiness to the Country, and was matter of fear least new Reprisals would be made on the out skirts; wherefore it was determined that Collonel *Walton* with one hundred and eighty Men should go to *Penobscot* and the adjacent Territories, where he burnt two Fishing Vessels (that were preparing to come upon us early in the Spring) and took several Captives, with some Plunder.

But *New-England* at this time was not alone insulted. The *Jesuits* were every way endeavouring to stir up the *Indians*, and at last did influence them to make a descent on the Borders of *Virginia*, where they murdered a great many of the *Palatines*: Upon which a considerable Number was raised, who went in quest of them,

and

and destroyed four *Towns*, besides a great many whom they took Prisoners. Some of them were supposed to be the *Senakees*, who are a Branch of the *Five Nations*. Another Tribe called the *Shacktaus*, made many Incursions on *Carolina*; upon which Col. *Gibs* the Governour commissionated Capt. *Hastings* and B—— the *Indian* Emperour, who was in League with the *English*; as also Capt. *Welch*, with the Assistance of the *Chicksha* Indians, to fall on them in several parts, and in a little time got to their Head-quarters, where the Enemy in three Divisions endeavoured to surround them, but after a smart Engagement, received a perfect Overthrow; which was followed with the burning and destroying four hundred Houses or Wigwams. The Friend *Indians* appeared bold and active, but for want of Discipline and a good Regulation, did not the Service that otherwise they might. After this Col. *Barnwell* went in pursuit of another Nation call'd the *Tuskarorahs*, and entirely routed them.

I now return to our Fronties, where at *Exeter*, *April* 16th. 1712. they kill'd Mr. *Cuningham* as he was travelling the Road from Mr. *Hilton*'s to *Exeter*: After that they shot *Samuel Webber*, between *York* and Cape *Neddick*: Others fell on several Teams in *Wells*, where they slew three & wounded as many more. One of the slain was Lieut. *Littlefield*, who a little before was redeemed out of Captivity, and a Person very much lamented. Soon after they appeared in the middle of the Town, and carried away two from thence. They went to *Spruce Creek*, where they kill'd a Boy and took another, and then went to *York*, but being
pur-

pursued made their escape. Another Party fell on the upper branch of *Oyster-River*, where they shot *Jeremiah Cromett*, and three Miles higher burnt a Saw-mill with a great many thousand of Boards. Next day they slew *Ensign Tuttle* at *Tole-End*, and wounded a Son of Lieut. *Herd*'s as he stood Sentinel. *May* 14th about thirty *French* and *Indians* who had a design on *York*, surpriz'd a *Scout* of ours as they were marching to *Cape-Neddick*, where they slew Sergant *Nalton*, and took seven besides: the remainder fought on a retreat till they got to a Rock, which for some time prov'd a good Barrier to them, and there continued untill they were releived, by the Vigilant Care of Capt. *Willard*. About this time fifty of our *English* who went up *Merrimack-River* returned, with the good Account of eight *Indians* that they had slain, and of considerable Plunder besides which they had taken, without the loss of one Man.

June 1st they again came to *Spruce-Creek*, where they shot *John Pickernell* as he was locking his door, and going to the Garrison; they also wounded his Wife and knockt a Child on the head, which they Scalpt, yet afterwards it recovered. Two days after they were seen at *Amsbury*, then at *Kingstown*, where they wounded *Ebenezer Stephens*, and *Stephen Gilman*, the latter of which they took alive and inhumanely Murdered. After this they kill'd one at *Newchawanick*, and on *July* 18th. fell on a Company at *Wells*, where they slew another and took a *Negro* Captive, who afterwards made his Escape. The Sabbath after they endeavoured to intercept the People at *Dover* as they came from Worship; upon on which a Scout was fent in perfuit, but made no difcovery. Yet in the intermitting time they took two Children from Lieut. *Herd*'s Garrifon, and not having time to Scalp them, cut off both their Heads, and carried them away. There was not a Man at that time at home; however one *Eafter Jones* fupplied the place of feveral; for fhe couragioufly advanced the Watch-box, crying aloud, *Here they are, come on, come on*; which fo terrified them as to make them draw off, without doing any further Mifchief. The Enemy at this time were thought to be very numerous, for they appeared in many Parties, which occafioned an additional number to be left to cover the Frontiers, under the Command of Capt. *Davis*, whofe vigilant Care (thro' the bleffing of God on it) kept them from doing any further Mifchief: *September* 1ft they kill'd *John Spencer*, and wounded *Dependance Stover*. At this time a Sloop from *Placentia*, with forty five *French* and *Indians* was cruifing on our Coaft, which Capt. *Carver* obferving, gave her chafe, and took her: But our Fifhery at *Cape Sables*, thro' the defect of the Guard-Ship, were great Sufferers; where no lefs than twenty fell into their Hands.

The laft Action that happened (of any moment) this War, was at Mr. *Plaifted*'s Marriage with Capt. *Wheelwright*'s Daughter of *Wells*, where happened a great concourfe of People, who as they were preparing to mount in order to their return, found two of their Horfes miffing; upon which Mr. *Downing* with *Ifaac Cole* and others went out to feek them; but before they had gone many Rods, the two former were kill'd and the others

others taken. The Noise of the Guns soon alarm'd the Guests, and Capt: *Lane,* Capt. *Robinson* and Capt. *Herd,* with several others mounted their Horses, ordering twelve Soldiers in the mean time to run over the Field, being the nearer way: But before the Horsemen got far, they were ambush'd by another Party, who kill'd Capt. *Robinson,* and dismounted the rest; and yet they all escaped excepting the *Bridegroom,* who in a few days after was redeem'd by the prudent Care of his Father, at the Expence of more than three hundred Pounds. Capt. *Lane* and Capt. *Harmon* mustered what Strength they could, and held a dispute with them some time, but there was little or no Execution done on either side.

Not long after this we had advice of a *Suspension of Arms* between the *two Crowns,* which the *Indians* being apprized of, came in with a Flag of Truce and desired a *Treaty.* Their first Application was to Capt. *Moodey* at *Casco,* desiring that the Conferance might be there; but the *Governour* not willing so far to condesend, order'd it to be at *Portsmouth,* where they accordingly met *July* 11th. 1713. three Deligates from St. *John's,* three from *Kenebeck,* including the other Settlements from *Penecook, Amasecontee, Naridwalk, Saco,* and all other Adjacent Places; where Articles of Pacification were drawn up, which I have hereunto annexed. *viz.*

'Whereas for some Years last past we have
'made a breach of our Fidelity and Loyal-
'ty to the Crown of *Great Britain,* and have made
'open Rebellion against her Majesty's Subjects,
'the

'the *English* Inhabiting the *Massachusets*, *New-
'hampshire*, and other her Majesty's Territories
'in *New-England*; and being now sensible of the
'Miseries which we and our People are reduced
'unto thereby; We whose names are hereunto
'subscribed, being *Delegates* of all the *Indians* be-
'longing to *Naridgwalk*, *Narahamegock*, *Amase-
'contee*, *Pigwacket*, *Penecook*, Rivers of *St. John's*
'and *Merimack*, parts of her Majesty's Provinces
'of the *Massachusets-Bay*, and *New-Hampshire*,
'within her Majesties Soveraignty, having made
'Application to his Excellency *Joseph Dudley*,
'Esq. Captain General and Governour in Chief
'in and over the said Provinces, that the Trou-
'bles which we have unhappily rais'd or occasio-
'ned against her *Majesty*'s Subjects the *English*
'and our selves may cease and have an end; and
'that we may again enjoy her Majesty's Grace
'and Favour: And each of us respectivly for our
'selves, and in the Names and with the free Con-
'sent of all the *Indians* belonging to the several
'Places and Rivers aforesaid, and all other *Indi-
'ans* within the said Provinces of the *Massachu-
'sets-Bay*, and *New-Hampshire*, hereby acknow-
'ledging our selves the Lawful Subjects of our
'Sovereign Lady *Queen Anne*, and promising our
'hearty Submission and Obedience to the Crown
'of *Great Britain*, do solemnly Covenant Promise
'and Agree with the said *Joseph Dudley*, Gover-
'nour, and all such as shall be hereafter in the
'place of *Captain General* and Governour in Chief
'of the said *Provinces* and Territories on her Ma-
'jesty's behalf in form following; *That is to say*,
'That at all times forever from and after the date

'of these Presents, we will cease and forbear all acts of Hostility towards all the Subjects of *Great Britain*, and not offer the least Hurt or Violence to them or any of them in their Persons and Estates; but will henceforth hold and mainiain a firm and constant Amity and Friendship with all the *English*, and will never entertain any Treasonable Conspirasy with any other Nation to their disturbance: That her Majesty's Subjects the *English* shall and may quietly and peaceably enter upon, improve and forever enjoy all and singular the Rights of Land and former Settlements, Properties and Possessions within the the *Eastern* parts of said Provinces of the *Massachusets-Bay* and *New-Hampshire*, together with the Islands Inlets, Shores, Beaches and Fishery within the same, without any Molestation or Claim by us or any other *Indians*; and be in no wise Molested or disturbed therein; Saving unto the *Indians* their own Ground, and free liberty of Hunting, Fishing, Fowling, and all other Lawful Liberties and Priviledges, as on the eleventh day of *August* in the year of our Lord One thousand six hundred and ninety three: That for Mutual Safety and Benefit, all Trade and Comerce which hereafter may be allowed betwixt the *English* and the *Indians*, shall be only in such Places, and under such Management and Regulation, as shall be stated by her Majesty's Government of the said Provinces respectively.

'And to prevent Mischiefs and Inconveniencies, the *Indians* shall not be allowed for the present, or until they have liberty from the respective

'spective Goverments to come near unto any
'*English* Plantations or Settlements on this side of
'*Saco* River.

'That if any Controversy or Difference hap-
'pen hereafter, to and betwixt any of the *English*
'and the *Indians* for any real or supposed Wrong
'or Injury done on the one side or the other, no
'private Revenge shall be taken by the *Indians*
'for the same, but proprr Application shall be
'made to her Majesty's Goverments upon the
'place for remedy thereof in due course of Jus-
'tice; we hereby submiting our selves to be ru-
'led and governed by her Majesty's Laws, and
'desire to have the Protection and Benefit of the
'same.

'We confess that we have contrary to all Faith
'and Justice broken our Articles with Sir *William*
'*Phips*, Governour in the year of our Lord God
'1693. and with the *Earl of Bellamont* in the year
'1699.

'And the assurance we gave to his Excellency
'*Joseph Dudley* Esq in the year of our Lord God,
'1702. in the Month of *August*, and 1703. in the
'Month of *July*, notwithstanding we have been
'well treated by the said Governours. But we
'resolve for the future not to be drawn into any
'perfidious Treaty or Correspondance to the hurt
'of any of her Majesty's Subjects of the Crown
'of *Great Britain*; and if we know any such, we
'will seasonably reveal it to the *English*.

'Wherefore we whose Names are hereunto
'subscribed, Delegates for the several Tribes of
'*Indians* belonging to the River of *Kenebeck*, *Ame-*
'*rasacoggin*, St. *John's*, *Saco*, *Merimack*, and the
'parts

'parts adjacent, being sensibe of our great Offence
'and Folly in not complying with the aforesaid
'Submission and Agreements, and also the Suffer-
'ings and Mischiefs that we have thereby expos-
'ed our selves unto, do in all humble and submis-
'sive manner, cast our selves upon her Majesty
'for Mercy, and Pardon for all our past Rebelli-
'ons, Hostilities and violations, of our Promises;
'praying to be received unto her Majesty's Grace
'and Favour.

'And for and on behalf of our selves, and all
'other the *Indians* belonging to the several Rivers
'and Places aforesaid, within the Sovereignty of
'her Majesty of *Great Britain*, do again acknow-
'ledge, and confess our hearty and sincere Obe-
'dience unto the Crown of *Great Britain*, and do
'solemnly renew, and confirm all and every of
'the Articles and Agreements contained in the
'former and present Submission.

'This Treaty to be humbly laid before her
'Majesty for her Ratification and further Order.
'IN WITTNESS wereof we the Delegates a-
'foresaid, by Name *Kizebenuit, Iteansis,* and *Jac-
'koid* for *Penobscot, Joseph* and *Æneas,* for *St.
'John's, Warrueensu, Wadacanaquin,* and *Bomazeen*
'for *Kenebeck,* have hereunto set our hands and
'Seals this 13th. day of *July,* 1713.

Signed

(79)

Signed Sealed and delivered
in the presence of us,

Edmund Quinsey
Spencer Phips
Wil. Dudley
Shad. Walton
Josiah Willard
&c.

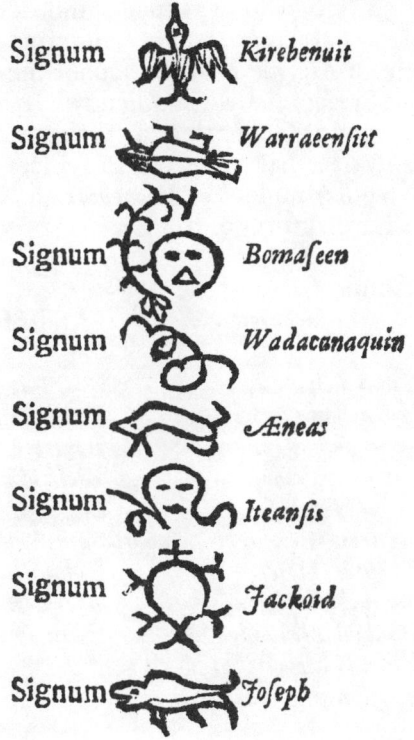

Signum Kirebenuit
Signum Warraeensitt
Signum Bomaseen
Signum Wadacanaquin
Signum Æneas
Signum Iteansis
Signum Jackoid
Signum Joseph

Province of New-Hampshire.

THe Submission & Pacification of the E*a*stern Indians was made and done the thirteenth Day of *July*, 1713. Annoque Regni Reginæ nunc *Magnæ Britaniæ* Duodecimo.

Present, his Excellency *Joseph Dudley*, Esq; Captain General and Governour in Chief, in and over her Majesty's Provinces of the *Massachusetts-Bay* and *New-Hampshire* in *New-England*, and Vice-Admiral of the same.

Councellours of the *Massachusetts*.   And of *New-Hampshire*.

Massachusetts	New-Hampshire
Samuel Sewall,	*Wil. Vaughan,*
Jonathan Corwin,	*Peter Coffin,*
Penn Townsend,	*Robert Elliot,*
John Appleton,	*Rich. Waldron,*
John Higginson,	*Nathan. Weare,*
Andrew Belcher, Esqrs.	*Sam. Penhallow,* Esqrs.
Thomas Noyes,	*John Plaisted,*
Samuel Appleton,	*Mark Hunking,*
Ichabod Plaisted,	*John Wentworth.*
John Wheelwright,	
Benjamin Lynde.	

For a further Ratification of this Treaty, several Gentlemen of both Governments went from *Portsmouth* to *Casco*, where a great Body of *Indians* were assembled, to know the Result of matters; It being a Custom among them on all such Occasions, to have the whole of their Tribes present;

sent; having no other Record of conveying to Posterity, but what they communicate from Father to Son, and so to the Son's Son. When the several Articles were read and explained, by Interpreters upon Oath, (the Delegates being present) they signified an unanimous Consent and Satisfaction, by loud Huzza's and Acclamations of Joy: Many Presents were then made them, which were thankfully received, and every Tribe had their proportion given out; but they were so disorderly, that *Mauxis* (altho' he was the chief *Sagamore* in all the *Eastern* parts) was rob'd by the Morning of all he had; upon which he made a miserable Complaint unto the *English* next Day, of the unruliness of his young Men, who had stollen away all he had, therefore beg'd a new Supply. But altho' their Government is so *Anarchical*, and their Chiefs have so little Respect and Honour shewn them, yet in their Council they observe a very excellent Decorum; not suffering any to speak but one at a time; which is deliver'd with such a remarkable Pathos, and surprizing Gravity, that there is neither Smile nor Whisper to be observed, until he that speaks has finish'd his Discourse, who then sits down, and after that another riseth up.

The Peace thus concluded and so firmly ratified, gave matter of Encouragment to the *Eastern* Inhabitants for re-settling their former Habitations; who were also countenanced and assisted by the Government, even from *Cape-Porpas* to *Kenebeck* River, where several Gentlemen who had large tracts of Land, granted a hundred Acres to

M every

every one for Encouragment that would go and Settle; supporting a Minister besides (for some time) and employ'd a Sloop at their own Charge for carrying and re-carrying the Inhabitants, with their Stock; which gave so great Encouragment, that several Towns began to be settled, as *Bromswick, Topsham, Augusta, George Town,* &c. In which a great many fine Buildings were erected, with several *Saw-mills,* &c.

A *Fishery* was also undertaken by the ingenious *Docter Noyes,* where twenty Vessels were employ'd at a time. He afterwares built a stone Garrison at *Augusta* at his own Charge, which was judged to be the best in the *Eastern* Country; and for a while was kept at the publick Cost, but afterwards slighted; which occasioned the Inhabitants to with draw, and then the *Indians* burnt it with several other Houses;

In *Kenebeck* River the *Sturgeon Fishery* was also begun and carried on with so great Success, that many thousand Caggs were made in a Season; and esteemed as good as any that ever came from *Hambrough* or *Norway*; Besides vast quantities of Pipe Staves, Hogshead and Barrel, Pine Boards, Plank, and Timber of all sorts, which were not only transported to *Boston,* but to foreign places; Husbandry also began to thrive, and great stocks of Cattel were rais'd.

The *French Missionaries* perceiving the Growth of these Plantations, soon animated the *Indians* to disrest them, by insinuating that the Land was theirs, and that the *English* invaded their Properties; which was a vile and wrong Suggestion, for that their Conveyance were from the Ancient

Saga-

Sagamores, at least seventy Years before; and the Proprietors did not settle so high up by several Miles as was formerly possest be their Predecessours.

However the *Indians* could not be satisfied, but so threatned the Inhabitants, that many withdrew, and others were discouraged from going to Settle. Soon after they kill'd many of their Cattel, and commited many other Outrages.

No sooner was this Advice brought unto his Excellency, *Samuel Shute* Esq. who was now Captain General and Governour in Chief, in and over the Provinces of the *Massachusets-Bay*, and *New-Hampshire*, &c. (and one zealously affected for the Interest of the Country) but he appointed a Congress at *Arowsick* in *Kenebeck* River, in *August* 1717. where a great number of *Indians*, with the Chiefs of every Tribe accordingly met. And some of the Principal Gentlemen of both Provinces accompanied his *Excellency* to the place appointed. The Complaints on each side being impartially heard and debated, the Original Deeds from the Ancient *Sagamores* were produced and explained; having interpreters on Oath. The Articles drawn up and signed in the year 1713. were again read and ratified, to the seeming Satisfaction of the Principal *Sachems*, who inclined to Peace; and imputed the late Miscarriages unto the young Men, but were now resolved on a firm Harmony, and would in no respect violate the former Treaties. Upon this his *Excellency* made them several Presents, which they thankfully received, and in acknowledgment thereof, returned him a Belt of *Wampam*, with some Beavour Skins:

After this they drank the Kings Health, and promis'd Allegience to the Crown of *Great Britain*; so that every thing had now the promising Aspect of a lasting Peace. One thing I cannot here omit; three days after our departure, a number of *Indians* went a Duck hunting, which was a season of the year that the old ones generally shed their Feathers in, and the young are not so well flusht as to be able to fly; they drove them like a flock of Sheep before them into the Creeks, where without either Powder or Shot they kill'd at one time four thousand and six hundred; for they followed them so close that they knockt them down with Billets and Paddles, and sold a great number of them to the *English* for a Penny a dozen, which is their practice yearly, tho' they seldom make so great a Slaughter at once. But before two years were expired, they again began to insult the Inhabitants, being spur'd on by the *Jesuits*, which occasioned a *Scout* of fifty or sixty Men to be sent out, who kept them in some awe. But in the year 1720. they began to be more insolent, and appear'd in greater Bodies; upon which Collonel *Walton* was ordered with about two hundred Men to guard the Frontiers, and was after that appointed with Capt. *Moody, Harman Penhallow*, and *Wainright* to send to their Chiefs for Satisfaction for the late Hostilitys which they had done in killing the Cattle, &c. The *Indians* fearing the event promis'd to pay two hundred Skins, and for their fidelity to deliver up four of their young Men as Hostages. After this they became tolerably quiet, but in the Spring grew as insolent as before; especially in

Kene-

Kenebeck, where some time in *July* they came with ninety Canoos on *Padishals* Island, which lies opposite to *Arowsick*, and sent to speak with Capt. *Penhallow*, who fearing an intreague, refused. Upon which one hundred and fifty of them went over to him, with whom he held a Conference; especially with Mounsieur *Delachase*, and *Sabastian Ralle* who were *Jesuits*; Mounsieur *Croizen* from *Canada*, and St *Casteen* from *Penobscot* came also along with them, who brought a Letter for *Governour Shute* in behalf of the several Tribes, importing, That if the *English* did not remove and quit their Land in three weeks, they would burn their Houses and kill them as also their Cattle. Upon this an additional Number of Soldiers were sent under the command of Collonel *Thaxter* and Lieut. Col. *Goff*; and several Gentlemen of the Council were also appointed to enquire into the ground of these Tumults, and if possible to renew the Pacification; who accordingly went and sent Scouts to call the *Indians* in, but they slighted the Message with derision. Hereupon the Soldiers were order'd to continue, and reinforce the Garrisons that Winter. But in the Summer they renewed their insults, and on the thirteenth of *June* 1722 about sixty of them in twenty Canoos, came and took nine Families in *Merry meeting-Bay*, most of which they afterwards set at liberty, but sent Mr. *Hamilton, Love, Handson, Trescot* and *Edgar* to *Canada*; who with great difficulty and expence afterwards got clear. They then made a descent on St. *Georges*, where they burnt a Sloop, took several Prisoners, and fought the Garrison some time; and in a

Month

Month after came a greater Body from *Penobscot*, who kill'd five and engag'd the Fort twelve Days; being very much encouraged by the influence of the *Fryar* that was with them. But finding they could make no great impression, endeavoured to undermine it, and had made a considerable progress therein, till upon the falling of much Rain, the Trenches caved in, which caused the seige to break up, with the loss of twenty of them in the Engagment, as we were afterwards informed. About the same time Capt. *Samuel* with five others boarded Lieut. *Tilton*, as he lay at Anchor a fishing near *Damaris Cove*: They pinion'd him and his Brother, and beat them very sorely: But at last one got clear and released the other; who then fell with great Fury upon the *Indians*, threw one over-board, and mortally wounded two more.

Capt. *Savage*, Capt. *Blin*, and Mr. *Newton*, who at this time were coming from *Annapolis*, and knew nothing of their Ravages, went into *Passamaquady* for Water. They were no sooner ashore, but found themselves hem'd in by a Body of *Indians*, the *French* basely standing by and suffering it. They wanted to divide the Cargo of the Sloop among them, and at last sent Capt. *Savage* on board to procure some *Ransome*. But the Wind rising, he was forc'd off, and made the best of his way to *Boston*: Those that he left (after some Difficulty and Expence) were released.

Capt. *Harmon* who was now in *Kenebeck*, went up the River with a Detachment of thirty four Men, and seeing some Fires, went ashore in the Night, where he came on eleven Canooos: The
Indians

Indians were lying round the Fire, and so wearied, by much Dancing the day before upon the Success they had, that they stumbled over them as they lay asleep. Reports were various as to the number of *Indians* that were then slain; some say eighteen, others not so many: However they brought away fifteen Guns; and at a little distance found the Hand of an *Englishman* laid on the stump of a Tree, and his Body mangled after a barbarous manner; having his Tongue, Nose and private parts cut off: They brought away the Body, and gave it a decent Burial. It was found to be the Body of *Moses Eaton* of *Salisbury*.

In this brave attempt of Capt. *Harmon*, which was effected in ten minutes, we lost not one Man, yet at the same time a great Body of *Indians* lay near, who being startled at the Noise that was made, arose and fired several Guns, but did no Damage.

The Country at this time was in a surprizing Ferment, and generally disposed to a War; but the *Governour* and *Council* could not readily come into it, considering the vast Expence and Effusion of Blood that would unavoidably follow: Besides some were not satisfied with the Lawfulness of it at this time: For altho' they believed the *Indians* to be very criminal in many respects, yet were of Opinion that the *English* had not so punctually observed the Promises made to them of Trading-houses for the benefit of Commerce and Traffick, and for the preventing of Frauds and Extortions, too common in the private dealings of the *English* with them. But the grand abuse to them is the selling of strong Drink to them,

them, which has occasioned much quarreling and Sin and the loss of many Lives, to the great Scandal of Religion, and reproach of the Country. His *Excellency* was sensible of the Promises that he made them at the Treaty of Pacification; which he failed not to lay before the General Assembly; but he met with so much opposition that nothing could be effected. The firing an *Armourer* at the Publick Charge, was also engaged, but nothing done therein; So that the *Indians* were full of resentments, and thought themselves wrong'd. Yet all this time they made no application unto the Government for redress, which they ought to have done by the Articles of Agreement, but broke forth into Horrid and cruel Outrages, by burning killing and destroying. At last the *Governour* by repeated Addresses from the People, was obliged to call the *Council* together to concert what was proper to be done, who advised, to the proclaiming an open War. But their not cosulting before-hand with the other *Governments* was certainly a great oversight; who probably would have come into it, and thereby have help'd to support the Charge, which now lay wholly on the *Massachusetts* and *Newhampshire*.

Proclamation.

'WHereas the *Indians* inhabiting the *Eastern*
' parts of this *Province*, notwithstanding
' their repeated Submissions to his *Majesty*'s
' Crown and Goverment, their publick and so-
'lemn

'lemn Treatys and engagments, entred into with
' the Government here eſtabliſhed, to demean
' themſelves peaceably and amicably towards his
' Majeſty's good Subjects of this Province; and
' notwithſtanding the kind and good Treatment
' they have received from the Government, have
' for ſome Years laſt paſt appeared in conſiderable
' Numbers in an hoſtile manner, and given diſtur-
' bance to 'his Majeſty's Subjects, in the *Eaſtern*
' parts of this Province, killing their Cattel and
' threatning deſtruction to their Perſons and E-
' ſtates; and in abuſe of the Lenity and Forbear-
' ance of the Government, have lately with the ut-
' moſt Injuſtice and Treachery proceeded to
' plunder, deſpoil, and take Captive many of his
' Majeſty's good Subjects, to aſſault, take, burn, &
' deſtroy Veſſels upon the Seacoaſts, and Houſes
' and Mills upon the Land; to wound ſome, and
' in a moſt barbarous, and cruel manner to Mur-
' ther others, of the Inhabitants of this Province;
' and in a way of open Rebellion and Hoſtility to
' make an Audacious and furious aſſault upon
' one of his Majeſty's Forts when the King's Co-
' lours were flying

' I do therefore by and with the advice of his
' Majeſty's Council, hereby declare and proclaim
' the ſaid *Eaſtern Indians*, with their Confederates,
' to be Robbers, Traitors and Enemies to his
' Majeſty King *George*, his Crown and Dignity;
' and that they be henceforth proceeded againſt
' as ſuch: Willing and Requiring all his Maje-
' ſty's good Subjects, as they ſhall have Oppor-
' tunity, to do and execute all acts of Hoſtility
' againſt them; Hereby alſo forbidding all his

'Ma-

'Majesty's good Subjects to hold any Correspon-
'dence with the said *Indians*, or to give Aid,
'Comfort, Succour or Relief unto them, on pe-
'nalty of the Laws in that case made and pro-
'vided. And whereas there be some of the said
'*Indians* who have not been concerned in the
'perfidious and barbarous Acts beforementioned,
'and many may be desirous to put themselves
'under the Protection of this Government:

'To the intent therefore that utmost Clemen-
'cy may be shewn to such, I do hereby grant
'and allow them to come in and render them-
'selves to the commanding Officer of the Forces,
'or to the respective Officer of any Party or
'Parties in the Service; provided it may be with-
'in forty Days from this Time. And to the in-
'tent that none of our Friend *Indians* may be ex-
'posed, or any Rebels or Enemy *Indians* may
'escape on pretence of being Friends; I do
'hereby strictly forbid any of the said *Indians* to
'move out of their respective Plantations, or
'such other places whereto they shall be assign-
'ed, or to come into any *English* Town or Di-
'strict, within the Colony of the *Massachusetts-
'Bay* or the County of *York*, without being at-
'tended with such Men as I shall appoint to
'oversee them, at their peril, and as they tender
'their own safety. And further, I forbid all the
'Friend *Indians* to hold Communion with, har-
'bour or conceal any of the said Rebels, or Ene-
'my *Indians*; requiring them to seize and secure
'all such that may come among them, and to
'deliver them up to Justice.

'And

'And all Military Commission-Officers are
'hereby authorized and commanded to put this
'Declaration and Order in Execution.

Given at the Council-Chamber in Boston, *the twenty fifth of* July, 1722.

SAMUEL SHUTE.

Josiah Willard, Secr.

GOD Save the King.

The abovesaid Declaration (for substance) was also given out the Week after, at the Council-Chamber at *Portsmouth*, in the Province of *Newhampshire*.

Now altho' the Settlements in *Kenebeck* were the first that were molested, yet it's not to be supposed that the bent of the Enemies Fury was on them alone, as some would insinuate; for at the same time they interrupted the Fishery throughout all *Nova-Scotia*; many have reflected on the Government for suffering a Fort to be at St. *Georges*, as if that did irritate the *Indians*; but why the Proprietors might not make an improvment thereof, as well as any others on their right of Purchase I know not; considering that it was granted from the Crown, and no exemption made at the Treaty of Peace. Yet at the same time I must be free to say, that there was too great indulgence at first in the Government in suffering so many Townships at so great a distance to be laid out at once, unless they were more peopled; which has since been the occasion not only of a vast Expence, but a great effusion of Blood.

The number of Vessels were about sixteen which the Enemy took at *Canso*, as they went into the Harbours for their Necessity; which so soon as Governour *Philipps* was apprised of, he summoned the several Masters ashore with the Sailors, and proposed the fitting out of two Sloops well Man'd for recovering the Vessels and Captives, which being approved of, he forthwith ordered the Drums to beat for Volunteers, and in less then half a day fix'd them out with about twenty Men in each, under the command of Capt. *Eliot* and Capt. *Robinson*, who freely offered their services; but as Capt. *Eliot* out sail'd the other, he got first to a Harbour call'd *Winpague*, where he discovered some Vessels, and bore directly down upon them, 'till he came pretty near. The *Indians* being flush't with Success, and having thirty nine on board one of the Vessels which they had took, and seeing no more Men on board the *English* then what was usual, commanded them to strike for that they were their Prize. Unto whom Capt. *Eliot* reply'd that he was hastning to them; and in an instant called his Men on Deck, who fired on them with a loud Huzza, and clapt them on board; which was so surprising a Salutation, that they made a most dreadful yelling. However they resisted so well as they could for about half an hour, in which time Capt. *Eliot* received three Wounds, when Mr. *Broadstreet*, who commanded the Soldiers, entred
with

with Hand-*Granado*'s, moſt of the *Indians* jumpt over-board, who were ſhot in the Water. Thoſe that ran down in the hold, were tore in pieces by the Shells, ſo that only five eſcaped, who were wounded. One of our Men was kill'd, and ſeveveral hurt, particularly the Corporal of the Troops, who had five Swan-ſhot in his Body. Capt. *Eliot* being ill of his Wounds, was oblig'd to return, carrying with him ſeven Veſſels into *Canſo*, which he retook with fifteen Captives, ſix hundred Quintals of Fiſh, and two heads of the Chiefs of thoſe *Indians* that were among them. Upon this the Governour ordered the ſame Sloop back with a freſh ſupply of Men to reinforce Capt. *Robinſon*, who in a Week after brought in two *Indian* Scalps, a Scooner and a Sloop which they took at *Mallegaſh*.

After that he met with a *French* Man and an *Engliſh* Captive, who informed of a Body of *Indians* and five Veſſels that lay at a little diſtance, which he immediately went in purſuit of; but fearing the event, was not willing at firſt to engage them, but kept at ſome diſtance, and then three Canoos with three *Indians* in each double arm'd drew near, one of which came on board, as the reſt lay on their Paddles, whom tney treated friendly in expectation of a greater Prize. But the *Indian* growing jealous attempted to eſcape, and preſented his Gun to Lieut. *Jephſon*'s breaſt, which he putting by, ſhot him dead. Upon this they fir'd upon thoſe in the Canoos, and kill'd three. The Enemy was ſo numerous aſhore, that he thought it not ſafe to encounter them; however he took one Veſſel. At this

time

time they had twenty of our *English* Captives, but could not come to a fair Capitulation about their Redemption. However the Captain warn'd them to use them well, for as we had thirty of theirs at *Annapolis,* twenty at *Boston,* and as many more at *Canso,* as they treated ours, so we would theirs. Mr. *Broadstreet* now steer'd to the *Westward* of the Harbour where Capt. *Eliot* had the dispute before mentioned, where he retook three Vessels more, but could see neither Captive nor *Indians.* The Day after Capt. *Blin* very happily arrived with a Flag of Truce, and redeem'd seven Vessels and twenty four Captives, who otherwise would have been put to Death. From thence he sail'd to the *Cape,* and in his returning back, took three or four *Indians,* which he carried to *Boston.* Capt. *Southack* being inform'd of a small Body that was then at *Astagenash* in the Gulph of St. *Lawrence,* where Monsieur *Golden* the famous *Fryar* did reside, had an intent to visit him; but in his passage thro' the Gutt was happily diverted, where meeting with two Canoos, in which were six *Indians* he kill'd one, and took the other five.

The *General Assembly* not finding the former Bounty sufficiently encouraging to Volunteers, now pass'd an Act of *one hundred pounds* a Scalp to all such as supported themselves, and whoever was subsisted by the Publick, should have *sixty pounds* for the like: That any Company or Troop issuing forth upon an Alarm, should over and above the Establishment have *thirty pounds,* and an encouraging Reward besides, for all Prisoners that they took; and whatever Plunder might be taken should be shared among them: And if any Volunteers

lunteers or detach'd Soldiers should happen to be wounded or maimed in the Service, that during the continuance of such Wound or Maim, he shall be allowed such a Stipend or Pension as the *General Court* should think fit to order.

September the 10th we had a surprizing Account from *Arowsick* of *four or five hundred, Canada* and *Cape Sable Indians,* that fell upon them early in the Morning, who probably would have laid all desolate, had they not been seasonably discovered by a small Guard which Capt. *Penhallow* was sending out for assisting the Neighbourhood to gather in the Corn; who kill'd one and wounded three more of the Company: The report of which Guns did so alarm the Inhabitants, that they with most of their Substance got seasonably into the Garrison. Their first appearance seemed terrible, considering their Number, with the fewness of those that were to defend; who fought the Garrison some time, and shot *Samuel Brooking* thro' a Port-hole, after that they had kill'd fifty head of Cattle, and burnt twenty six dwelling Houses. The same Day in the Evening came Col. *Walton* and Capt. *Harmon,* with about thirty Men in two Whale-boats, who with those of Capt. *Temple* and *Penhallow*'s Men, (that could be spared out of the Garrisons) made about *seventy,* and gave them Battle some time: But the Enemy were so numerous, that they were like to have hem'd them in, had they not fought upon a retreat.

In the Night they drew off, without much cause of Triumph, and went up the River, where they attackt Mr. *Stratton,* as he was turning down in his Sloop, whom they mortally wounded; then went to *Richmond*, where some time they held a dispute with the Garrison, and afterwards drew off. The last that fell this Season was a Man at *Berwick*.

His *Excellency's* Affairs now calling him to *Great Britain*, the Government of the *Massachusetts* was wholly devolved on the Honourable *William Dummer*, Esq. Lieut. Governour; during whose Administration, there were as many remarkable Turns of *Divine Providence*, (respecting the Enemy) as have happened since the War commenc'd; whose Prudence and good Conduct have made him acceptable unto all.

The first Alteration that he made, was in Commissionating Col. *Westbrook* as Chief in the *Eastern* Affairs; who on the 10th of *February* march'd to *Penobscot*, and Capt. *Harmon* at the same time up *Amanascoggin* River, but neither of them had any Success, save burning their *Chappel* and some *Wigwams*. Capt. *Sayward* with a Company of Volunteers went as far as the *White Hills*, near one hundred miles into the Enemies Country, but met with the like misfortune.

So soon as the Spring advanced, they began to appear as furious as ever. At *Scarborough* they kill'd *Thomas Laribie* and his Son; after that Mrs. *Dering* and two Soldiers, where they also took *Mary Scamond*, *John Hunuel* and *Robert Jordan*. Another Party came to *Cochecha*, where they slew *Tristram Head*, *Joseph Ham*, and carried three Children Captive: From thence they went to *Lamper-Ele River*, where they kill'd *Aaron Rawlins* with one of his Children, carrying away his
Wife

Wife and three more with them. At *Northfield* they shot two, and meeting with the Reverend Mr. *Willard* of *Rutland*, they laid violent Hands upon him; but he being a Person of *Courage* agreeable to his *Strength*, he slew one and wounded another, till at last they gave him the fatal stroke. Two of Ensign *Stephens*'s Sons were also kill'd, and two more carried Captive.

Capt. *Watkins*, who at this time was engaged on a Fishing Voyage at *Canso*, was surprised by a small Body in the Night while abed. The Day before he was at Church, and it hapned that *two Ministers* in two different Congregations preached on one and the *same Subject*; namely, *preparing for sudden Death*; not knowing how soon or in what manner Death would attack them. His Lodging was on an *Island* at a little distance from the *Fort*; and altho' he was so strongly importun'd by several of his Friends to stay with them that Night, as if they had a secret impulse of some impending Evil; yet all the Arguments they could use, could no ways prevail nor influence him. He was a Gentleman of singular good Temper, respected and lamented by all that knew him. *John Drew* of *Portsmouth* (a pretty Youth) was slain with him, at the same time.

The Delegates of the six Nations of *Iroquoise*, with the *Mohegan* and *Scatacook* Indians, being disposed to come to *Boston*, were kindly entertained there. And at a Conference with the *General Assembly*, signified a great concern for the Blood that was so often shed by their Kinsmen and Brethren; That from the Original they were Friends to the *English*, and as a Testimony of
their

their continuing so, presented a belt of *Wampam*; which according to their Custom, is the renewing the Covenant. His Honour the *Lieut. Governour*, as an acknowledgement, gave each of them a piece of *Plate*, with Figures engraven thereon, as a *Turtle*, a *Bear*, a *Hatchet*, a *Wolf*, &c. which were the *Escutcheons* of their several Tribes. And the more to oblige them to our Interest, they had a promise made of *one hundred pounds* a Scalp for every *Indian* that they kill'd or took; which seem'd so pleasing to them, that they manifested a readiness of taking up the Hatchet in favour of the *English*, whenever any Hostility was made agaist them. After this they were entertained with the curious sight of a Gun that was made by the ingenious Mr. *Pim* of *Boston*; which altho' loaden but *once*, yet was discharg'd *eleven* times following with Bullets in the space of two minutes; each of which went thro' a double Door at fifty yards distance. They were then presented with an *Ox*, which with Bows and Arrows they kill'd and dress'd according to their own Custom; where thousands of Spectators were present to behold and hear their barbarous Singing and Dancing. But notwithstanding this free and generous Entertainment, with the firm promises they made of falling on our Enemies, (whenever they made any Insults on us) all proved of little or no Significancy; which was principally owing to the powerful influence of the *Dutch*, for the sake of Trade and Comerce with them, as was observed on the like Occasion.

October

October the thirteenth we had an account from *Northfield*, of a Body of *Indians* that fell on the Town-Fort, where they wounded two and kill'd as many more. Soon after they surprized Mr. *Cogshel* and his Boats Company as they were going ashore at *Mount Desart*.

December 25th about sixty laid siege to St. *Georges* Garrison, where they continued thirty Days, and were not a little flusht with the expectation of Success; for at their first coming they took two Soldiers, who gave an account of the state of Matters: But Mr. *Canady* the commanding Officer being one of uncommon Courage and Resolution, stood his Ground till Col. *Westbrook* arrived, who soon put them to a rout. After this some came to *Berwick*, where they took a Soldier as he was carelesly wandering from the Garrison.

The favourableness of the Winter prevented our marching to any of their Head quarters this Season, excepting to *Narridgwalk*, where Capt. *Moulton* found a vile and pernicious Letter from the Governour of *Quebeck*, directed unto the *Fryar*, exhorting him to push on the *Indians* with all imaginable Zeal against the *English*, whose Advice he as industriously pursued.

April 17th 1724. they shot *William Mitchel* of *Scarborough*, as he was plowing in the Field, and took two of his Sons, who afterward were released at the taking of *Narridgwalk*. They then fell on a Sloop at *Kenebunk*, which belong'd to *Lyn*, and kill'd the whole Company: But the greatest stroke was on Capt. *Winslow*, who with sixteen Men in two Whale-boats, went from St. *George's*

George's to the *Green-Islands*, where the Enemy usually frequent on the account of Fowling But on their return they were ambuscaded by two or three Companies of them that lay on each side the River. The first that fell was Sergeant *Harvey*, who commanded the other Boat; for by keeping too near the Shore, he gave the Enemy the greater Advantage: However he returned the Shot with as much bravery as could be expected, till overpower'd by a multitude. Capt. *Winslow*, who was considerably a-head and out of danger, perceiving the Engagement, couragiously return'd back to their Assistance. But before he could give them any relief, was surrounded with about *thirty* Canoos, who made a hideous yelling; but he gave them no answer but from the muzzles of his Guns. A smart Engagement followed, which held till Night: When finding his Thigh broken, and most of his Men slain, was oblig'd to hasten ashore; but there also he found himself unhappily way-laid: They fell on him with utmost fury, yet his Courage continued until the last; for (as one of those that escaped has since reported) he rested himself on his other Knee, and kill'd an *Indian* before they had power to flay him. Thus died that worthy *young Gentleman*, for the Cause of his Country. He was one of liberal Education and good Extract, being the Grand Son of Governour *Winslow* of *Plymouth*; and if he had survived, might have been of good Service in his Generation. *Sylvanus Nock*, a worthy Elder of the Church of *Oyster-River*, soon after this was slain as he was on Horseback. *Myles Thomson* of *Berwick* was the

same

same day also kill'd by another Party, and his Son was carried Captive. A few Days after they again beset Capt. *Penhallow*'s Garrison, where they took three as they were driving their Cows to Pasture, and at their drawing off kill'd a great many Cattle. Another Company fell on *Kingstown*, where they took *Peter Colcard*, *Ephraim Severns*, and two of Mr. *Stephens*'s Children, whom they carried to *Canada*; but by the unwearied Pains and Expence of Mr. *Stephens*, he in a little time purchased his Children. *Colcard* about six Months after made his escape and got unto his Friends, but did not survive long. *May* 24th they shot *George Chesley* as he was returning from publick Worship, with whom was *Elizabeth Burnum*, who was mortally wounded. Three Days after they went to *Perpooduck*, where they kill'd one and wounded another, and then march'd to *Saco*, where they slew *David Hill* a Friend *Indian*. On the same Day another Party went to *Chester*, where they took *Thomas Smith*, with another whom they pinion'd, but soon after they made their escape.

 The Frontiers being thus alarmed, two Companies of Volunteers went from *Newhampshire* on the Bounty Act *one hundred pounds* a Scalp, and it hapned that *Moses Davu*, as he was weeding his Corn, went unto a Brook to drink, where he saw three *Indian* Packs, upon which he informed the Troops that were then coming out. He with his Son went before as guides, but by an Ambushment were both shot dead. The *English* then fired on them, who kill'd one, and wounded two more, but could not find either of the latter,
altho'

altho' they track't them by their Blood some way. The Assembly of *New-Hampshire* then sitting, order'd the aforesaid Sum of one hundred pounds to be paid.

The next damage they did, was at *Groton*, but were so closely pursued, that they left several of their Packs behind. About which time News came to *Deerfield* of a Body of *Indians* discover'd up *Connecticut* River. Capt. *Thomas Wells* Rallied a Company of Men, and went in quest of them, but made no further Discovery, till, upon their return home, about four Miles from *Deerfield*, three of the Company (supposing themselves out of Danger) Rode at some distance before the rest, and unhappily fell into an Ambushment of the Enemy near a Swamp, and were all three kill'd by them. But the Company behind, hearing the Guns, rode up with all speed, and came upon the Enemy while they were scalping the slain; and firing upon them wounded several. Upon which the Enemy fled into the Swamp, and the *English* dismounting their Horses, ran in after them, and trackt them a considerable way by the Blood of the wounded, but found none. However they recovered ten Packs, and heard afterwards that *two* died of their Wounds, and a *third* lost the use of his Arm. Another Company fell on *Spurwink*, where they mortally wounded *Solomon Jordan*, as he was coming out of the Garrison. Next day being *July* the 18th. Lieut. *Bean* went in quest of them, and came up with a Scout of thirty whom he engag'd and put to flight, leaving twenty five Packs, twelve Blankets, a Gun, a Hatchet, and sundry other things behind them.

The

The Enemy not finding so great encouragment in attacking our Frontiers as they expected, were now resolved to turn *Pirates*, and accordingly intercepted several of our Fishery as they went in and out the Harbours for Wood, Water, or in case of Storms, and accordingly made up a Fleet of fifty Canoos, who design'd at first for *Monhegen*, but going thro' the Fox Islands, and seeing several Vessels at Anchor, surprized eight with little or no Opposition; in which were forty Men, twenty of whom they put to Death, reserving the Skippers and best Sailors to Navigate for them. After this they took fourteen more; & with the assistance of the *Cape Sable Indians*, became so powerful and desperate, that at first they terrified all Vessels that sail'd along the *Eastern* Shore. They then went to *St. Georges* with a design to burn that Garrison; in order whereto, they fill'd a couple of *Shallops* with cumbustible matter, which they set on fire, but it was happily extinguished. They then offered terms on surrendering which were rejected. And finding that neither Force nor Insinuation would prevail they withdrew, and sail'd to *Annapolis*, expecting to surprize the Fort; but firing at a Soldier in their March, gave an Alarm; and a detachment issued forth; who after a smart dispute gave them a perfect rout, but not without loss on our side.

The *Fishery* being thus invaded, two Shallops with about forty Men well fixt went from *Newhampshire*, who fairly came up with one of them, but thro' Cowardize and Folly were afraid to engage them: However Doctor *Jackson* from *Kittery*, and *Sylvanus Lakeman* from *Ipswich*, with a lesser number gave them Chase, and fired very smartly with their small Arms, altho' the Enemy had two great Guns and four Pateraroes, which cut their Shrouds and hindred their pursuit for some time: But being fixed again, they followed them with greater Resolution, and drove them into *Penobscot*, where a greater Body being ready to cover tuem, he was forced to desist. The Doctor and Mr. *Cutt* were dangerously wounded in this Engagement, but some time after recovered. This Storm of the Enemy by Sea produced no Calm ashore.

At *Rutland* they kill'd three Men, wounded one, and took another; and at *Oxford* beset a House that lay under a Hill, but as one of the Enemy attempted to break thro' the Roof, he was shot by a Woman of the House. The *Sabbath* now became a Day of Danger in which they often did Mischief, as at *Dover*, *Oyster-River* and *Berwick*, where they kill'd one, wounded a second, and carried away a third.

Capt. *Harmon*, *Moulton*, *Brown* and *Bene*, were now preparing for *Naridgwalk* with two hundred Men in seventeen Whale-boats. After they landed at *Triconnick*, they met with *Bomazeen* at *Bromswick*, (who had slain an *Englishman* some days before) whom they shot in the River, as he attempted to make an ascape. They afterwards kill'd his Daughter, and took his Wife Captive; who gave an account of the state of the Enemy, which encouraged them to march on briskly; and on *August* 12th they got within two miles of the place: Capt. *Harmon* drew off with about sixty Men to range their Corn fields, in hopes of
find-

finding some there, imagining they saw some Smokes; while Capt. *Moulton* with about an hundred Men moved forward, and when he came within view of the *Town*, artfully divided them into three Squadrons, of thirty in each; having ordered ten to guard their Baggage, and a Squadron on each Wing to lye in Ambush, while he with the like number encountered them in the Front. He went on with such Resolution, that he got within Pistol shot before he was discovered. The *Indians* were under amazing Terror; yet in their surprise some of them snatch'd up their Guns and fired: but their hands shook and they did no Execution. They immediately betook themselves to flight, and in running fell on the very muzzles of our Guns that lay in Ambush. Our Men pursued them so warmly, that several were slain on the spot; more got into their Canoos, & others ran into the River; which was so rapid and the falls in some places so great, that many of them were drowned. By this time Capt. *Harmon* came up, who was not so happy as to discover any of the Enemy where he expected. The number of the dead which we scalpt, were twenty six, besides Mounsieur *Ralle* the *Jesuit*, who was a Bloody Incendiary, and Instrumental to most of the Mischiefs that were done us, by preaching up the Doctrine of meriting Salvation by the destruction of *Hereticks*. Some say that Quarter was offered him, which he refused and would neither give nor take any. After this they burnt and destroyed the *Chappel*, Canoos, and all the Cottages that lay round, they also took four *Indians* alive, and recovered three Captives.

P   The

The number in all that were kill'd and drown'd were supposed to be eighty, but some say more; The greatest Victory we have obtained in the three or four last Wars; and it may be as noble an Exploit (all things considered) as ever hapned in the time of *King Phillip*. About seventy *French Mohawks* were now making a descent on our Frontiers, who divided into several Parties and kill'd a great number of Cattel. Some of them fell on the House of *John Hanson* of *Dover*, who being a stiff Quaker, full of Enthusiasm, and ridiculing the Military Power, would on no account be influenced to come into Garrison; by which means his whole Family (then at home,) being eight in number, were all kill'd and taken. But some time after his Wife and two or three of his Children were redeemed with considerable Pains and Expence.

September 4th. they fell on *Dunstable*, and took two in the Evening, next morning *Lieut. French* with fourteen Men went in quest of them; but being way-laid, both he and one half of his Company were destroyed. After that as many more of a fresh Company engaged them, but the Enemy being much superior in number overpower'd them, with the loss of one Man and four wounded.

On the *Monday* after they kill'd *Jabez Coleman* of *Kingstown*, with his Son, as they were gathering Corn-stalks. About the same time *Nathaniel Edwards* of *Northampton* was kill'd. And the next day the same Company of *Indians* went to *Westfield*, and fell on several People as they were coming out of the Meadows with their Carts loaden, and wounding one Man, had certainly taken him, but some of our Men bravely faced about, and attempted a shot upon them. But their Guns all missing fire except Mr. *Noah Ashley's*, his went off, and shot down one of the Enemy; which put a stop to their further pursuit of the *English* Hereupon a Company Rallyed, and went after the Enemy, and quickly found the *Indian* whom *Ashley* had slain. And taking his Scalp, said *Ashley* brought it to *Boston*, and received one hundred Pounds Reward for it. And now a Regiment of fresh Men under the Command of Col. *Westbrook* were preparing for *Penobscot*, one of their chief places of randevous for Planting and Fishing; but by the unskilfulness of his Guides, were led into a labyrinth of Difficulties, and after a long Fategue return'd without any discovery.

Capt. *Lovewell* from *Dunstable* with thirty Volunteers, at the same time went *North-ward*, who marching several Miles up the Country came on a *Wigwam* wherein were two *Indians*, one of which they kill'd and the other took, for which they received the promised bounty of *one hundred pounds* a Scalp, and *two Shillings and six pence* a day besides.

Other Companys were disposed to go out on the like encouragment, but did not see the track of an *Indian*; being under such amazing Terror, by reason of their late overthrow at *Naridgwalk*, that they deserted their former Habitation; for when Capt. *Heath* went to *Penobscot*, he made no other discovery than a few empty *Wigwams*.

The Government (being thorowly appriz'd of the perfidy of the *French* at *Canada*, in supplying the *Indians* with all necessary stores of War, notwithstanding the Peace at *Utrecht*, so firmly ratified between the two Crowns) sent Col. *Thaxter* and Col. *Dudley* from the *Massachusets*, with Mr. *Atkinson* from *New Hampshire*, as Commissioners to represent the many Grievances that arose thereby; As also to demand the several Captives which they had of ours, and that hence forward they would withdraw all manner of assistance from the Enemy; for as they were *Indians* bordering between both Governments, they belonged either to the Dominion of *Great Britain*, or unto the *French King*; if to the *French* King, then consequently they were his Subjects, and the encouraging or supplying them with warlike Stores against the *English*, was a flagrant violation of the *Peace* between the two *Crowns*; if they belonged to the King of *Great Britain*, then the exciting them to War was as great a breach, and a stiring them up to Rebellion, contrary unto their Allegiance and Submission in the year 1693. which was afterwards renewed in the year 1713. and 1717.

Our Gentlemen in their Journey to *Quebeck*, met the Governour at *Mount Real* unto whom they delivered this Message: Upon which the Governour seem'd to extenuate his supplying or countenancing them in any act of Hostility; till they made it evident from Letters under his Hand unto Mounsieur *Rallee* the *Jesuit* and Father Confessour. But to palliate the Matter he reply'd, They were an *Independant Nation*, and that as the

Cap-

Captives were out of his reach he would not engage therein. But as to those among the *French* he would order them to be released upon paying the first Cost that they had given the *Indians*. This we were oblig'd to do, after an exorbitant manner; and in the whole got but sixteen with the promise of ten more. Notwithstanding this he would often reflect on the *English* for invading the Properties of the *Indians*, till our Commissioners demonstrated that we possess'd no more than what we purchased, and had formerly inhabited; and in as much as the Boundaries between the *Two Crowns* were firmly fixt, that all the *Indians* inhabiting this side *L' Accadia*, must of consequence belong to the Crown of *Great Britain*. After this our Gentlemen departed, acknowledging the kind Entertainment which his *Excellency* had given them; who order'd a Guard to attend them part of their way home.

But the difficulties and hazards that they met with in their Journey were great and terrible. It took them full four Months. The Lake they passed over was a *hundred and fifty* miles long, and *thirty* wide, which was covered with Water four inches on the surface of the Ice. The first place they came to was *Shamblee*, where is a strong Fortification 200 foot square, and 30 foot high, with four Bastions, in which are four teer of Guns one above another. From thence they travelled to *Mount Real*, which is an Island of 30 miles long and 12 wide, lying in the middle of the River commonly called St. *Lawrence*'s River; about 180 miles up from *Quebeck*, navigable for Vessels of about 100 Tons. This City

(of

(of *Mount Real*) lies near the middle, walled round with Stone and Lime 16 foot high and 3 thick; but no Battery or Fortification; in which are three Churches, two Chappels, two Nunneries, and two Streets of three quarters of a mile in length; containing about 400 Houses. Their Trade is mostly in Furs, which they transport to *Quebeck*, and from thence to *France*.

Capt. *Lovewell*, who was endowed with a generous Spirit and Resolution of serving his Country, and well acquainted with hunting the Woods, raised a new Company of Volunteers, & marched some miles beyond their common Head-quarters: On the *Easterly* side of *Winnepissocay* Ponds he cross'd an *Indian* Track, and soon after espied two of them, whose Motions he watch'd all the Day, and at Night silently came upon them as they lay asleep round their Fire. At his first firing he kill'd *seven*, after that *two* more, and wounded another, which was their whole Company: Who being within a Day and halfs march of our Frontiers, would probably have done Mischief, had they not been so seasonably prevented. Their Arms were so new and good, that most of them were sold for *seven pounds* apiece, and each of tham had two Blankets, with a great many spare *Moggasons*, which were supposed for the supplying of Captives that they expected to have taken. The Plunder was but a few Skins; but during the March our Men were well entertained with *Moose*, *Bear*, and *Deer*; together with *Salmon Trout*, some of which were three foot long, and weighed *twelve pounds* apiece.

April

April 13th. 1725. there came two *Indians* to *Macquoit*, and took one *Cockram*, a Soldier of about eighteen years of Age, whom they carried thirty Miles into the Woods. The first night they pinioned him, but left him loose the second. He took an opportunity (as they were asleep,) to knock them both on the head, Scalpt 'em and brought their Scalps away with him, and their Guns. But in his return he was so unhappy as to loose a Gun, and one of the Scalps, in fording over a River. When he came to the Garrison and gave an account of the whole affair, there went out a Party the next Morning and found the *Indians* both dead according to the information that he had given He was not only rewarded according to the *Act*, but was advanced in his Post, for his brave Action, and for the encouragment of others.

On the *Monday* after came another Party to *Yarmouth*, where they slew *William* and *Mathew Scales*, which was a great weakning to that Garrison, being very active and industrious Men, and the principal supporters thereof.

After this they went to *Cape-Porpos* and way-laid Lieut. *Trescott* with some others, as they were passing along the Road, whom they fired on, and wounded the said *Trescott* in several places.

A Vessel from *Canso* about this time arriving, brought an account of seventy *Indians* that fell on an Out-house in view of the Garrison, where they kill'd seven Men, one Woman and a Child, and from thence went to Capt. *Durell*'s Island, where they beset a fortified House in which were only four, who engag'd them several Hours; one of of which was in a little time shot thro' a loophole, but the remaining three held out and defended themselves with such bravery, that the Enemy was obliged to draw off with considerable loss.

Capt. *Lovewell* being still animated with an uncommon zeal of doing what Service he could, made another attempt on *Pigwackett* with forty four Men; who in his going built a small Fort near *Ossipy*, to have recourse unto in case of danger, as also for the relief of any that might be sick or wounded; and having one of his Men at this time sick, he left the *Doctor* with eight Men more to guard him: With the rest of his Company he proceeded in quest of the Enemy, who on *May* the 8th about 10 in the Morning, forty miles from said Fort, near *Saco* Pond, he saw an *Indian* on a point of Land: Upon which they immediately put off their Blankets and Snapsacks, and made towards him; concluding that the Enemy were a-head and not in the rear. Yet they were not without some Apprehensions of their being discovered two days before, and that the appearing of one *Indian* in so bold a manner, was on purpose to ensnare them. Wherefore the Captain calling his Men together, proposed whether it was best to engage them or not; who boldly reply'd, *That as they came out on purpose to meet the Enemy, they would rather trust Providence with their Lives and die for their Country, than return without seeing them.* Upon this they proceeded and mortally wounded the *Indian*, who notwithstanding returned the Fire, and wounded Capt. *Lovewell* in the Belly: Upon which Mr. *Wyman* fired

fired and kill'd him. But their dismantling themselves at this juncture proved an unhappy snare; for the Enemy taking their Baggage, knew their strength by the number of their Packs, where they lay in ambush till they returned, and made the first shot; which our Men answered with much bravery, and advancing within twice the length of their Guns, slew nine: The Encounter was smart and desperate, and the Victory seem'd to be in our favour, till Capt. *Lovewell* with several more were slain and wounded, to the number of *twelve*: Upon which our Men were forced to retreat unto a Pond, between which and the Enemy was a ridge of Ground that proved a Barrier unto us. The Engagement continued ten hours, but altho' the shouts of the Enemy were at first loud and terrible, yet after some time they became sensibly low and weak, and their appearance to lessen: Now whether it was thro' want of Ammunition, or on the account of those that were slain and wounded, that the Enemy retreated; certain it is they first drew off and left the Ground: And altho' many of our Men were much enfeebled by reason of their Wounds, yet none of the Enemy pursued them in their return. Their number was uncertain, but by the advice which we afterwards received, they were *seventy* in the whole, whereof *forty* were said to be kill'd upon the spot, *eighteen* more died of their Wounds, and that twelve only returned. An unhappy instance at this time fell out respecting one of our Men, who when the Fight began was so dreadfully terrified, that he ran away unto the Fort, telling those who were there,

there, that Capt. *Lovewell* was kill'd with most of his Men; which put them into so great a Consternation, that they all drew off, leaving a bag of Bread and Pork behind, in case any of their Company might return and be in distress.

The whole that we lost in the Engagement were *fifteen*, besides those that were wounded. *Eleazer Davis* of *Concord* was the last that got in, who first came to *Berwick* and then to *Portsmouth*, where he was carefully provided for, and had a skilful Surgeon to attend him. The Report he gave me was, That after Capt. *Lovewell* was kill'd, and Lieut. *Farewell* and Mr. *Robbins* wounded, that Ensign *Wyman* took upon him the command of the shattered Company, who behaved himself with great Prudence and Courage, by animating the Men and telling them, *That the Day would yet be their own, if their Spirits did not flag*; which enliven'd them anew, and caused them to fire so briskly, that several discharged between twenty and thirty times apiece. He further added, that Lieut. *Farewell*, with Mr. *Fry* their Chaplain, *Josiah Jones*, and himself, who were all wounded, march'd towards the Fort; but *Jones* steer'd another way, and after a long fategue and hardship got safe into *Saco*. Mr. *Fry* three days after, thro' the extremity of his Wounds, began to faint and languish, and died. He was a very worthy and promising young Gentleman, the bud of whose Youth was but just opening into a Flower.

Mr. *Jacob Fullam*, who was an Officer and an only Son, distinguish'd himself with much bravery. One of the first that was kill'd was by his hand; and when ready to encounter a second,

it's

it's said, that he and his Adverſary fell at the very inſtant by each others Shot. Mr. *Farewell* held out in his return till the eleventh day; during which time he had nothing to eat but Water and a few Roots which he chewed; and by this time the Wounds thro' his Body were ſo mortified, that the Worms made a thorow Paſſage. The ſame day this *Davis* caught a Fiſh which he broil'd, and was greatly refreſh'd therewith; but the Lieut. was ſo much ſpent, that he could not taſte a bit. *Davis* being now alone in a melancholy deſolate ſtate, ſtill made toward the Fort, and next day came to it, where he found ſome Pork and Bread, by which he was enabled to return as before mentioned.

Juſt as I had finiſhed this Account, I ſaw the *Hiſtorical Memoirs* of the ingenious Mr. *Symmes*, wherein I find two things remarkable, which I had no account of before: One was of Lieut. *Robins*, who being ſenſible of his dying ſtate, deſired one of the Company to charge his Gun and leave it with him, being perſwaded that the *Indians* by the Morning would come and ſcalp him, but was deſirous of killing one more before he died. The other was of *Solomon Kies*, who being wounded in three places, loſt ſo much Blood as diſabled him to ſtand any longer; but in the heat of the Battle, calling to Mr. *Wyman* ſaid, he was a dead Man; however ſaid that if it was poſſible he would endeavour to creep into ſome obſcure hole, rather than be inſulted by theſe bloody *Indians*: But by a ſtrange Providence, as he was creeping away, he ſaw a Canoo in the Pond, which he roll'd himſelf into, and

and by a favourable Wind (without any assistance of his own) was driven so many miles on, that he got safe unto the Fort.

In 1 *Sam.* 31. 11, 12, 13. it is recorded to the immortal Honour of the Men of *Jabesh Gilead*, that when some of their renowned *Heroes* fell by the hand of the *Philistines*, that they prepared a decent Burial for their Bodies.

Now so soon as the Report came of Capt. *Lovewell*'s defeat, about fifty Men from *New-hampshire* well equipt, marched unto *Pigwackett* for the like end, but were not so happy as to find them: But Col. *Tyng* from *Dunstable*, with Capt. *White* who went afterwards, buried twelve; where at a little distance they found three *Indians*, among whom was *Paugus*, a vile and bloody Wretch. Now the reason why no more of the Enemy could be found, was because it's customary among them to conceal their dead, and bury them in some places of obscurity.

Give me leave here again to relate (as I did before respecting Col. *Hilton*) that six or eight Days before Capt. *Lovewell* was defeated, we had a current Report several miles round of his being so, with little or no variation both as to Time and Circumstances.

Our encountering the Enemy at such a distance was so terrible and surprizing, that they never found any body after. And tho' our Actions in this War can bear no comparison with those of our *British* Forces, (which have caused the World to wonder) yet not to mention the bravery of these Worthies, who died in the Bed of Honour, and for the interest of their Country,

try, would be a denying them the Honour that is due unto their Memory, and a burying them in Oblivion.

The mourning Drum, the Lance and Ensigns trail.
The Robes of Honour all in Sable vail,

Mr. *Wyman*, who distinguish'd himself in such a signal manner, was at his return presented with a Silver hilted Sword and a *Captains* Commission. *Edward Lingfield* was also made an Ensign, and the *General Assembly* (to shew a grateful Acknowledgment to the Soldiers, and a compassionate Sympathy unto the Widows and Orphans,) ordered the Sum of *fifteen hundred pounds* to be given them, under a certain regulation. And for a further encouragment of *Volunteers*, ordered *four Shillings* a day out of the Publick to be paid every one that would enlist, besides the bounty of *one hundred pounds a Scalp*. Upon which a great many brave Men under the Command of Capt. *White*, Capt. *Wyman*, and others went out, but the Extremity of the Heat prevented their Marching far. Many of them sickned of the Bloody Flux, and some dyed after their return; particularly Capt. *White* and Capt. *Wyman*, whose Deaths were very much lamented.

Saquarexis, and *Nebine*, one a Hostage and the other a Prisoner belonging to the *English*, being desirous of visiting their old Acquaintance, had liberty granted them on their *Parole*; who after some time returned and gave an Account, that the *Indians* were generally disposed to a *Peace*, for that the losses they met with, and the daily Terrour

rour they were under made their lives miserable. After this they went out again, and meeting with several others, they represented their ready desires of having a Treaty of *Pacification* with the *English*. Upon which Col. *Walton*, from *New-Hampshire*, Col. *Stoddard* and Mr. *Wainwright*, from the *Massachusets*, were appointed Commissioners to go unto *St. Georges* to hear and report what they had to offer. They arrived there *July* the second, and sent the said two *Indians* with a Letter unto their Chiefs, letting them know that they were come; who in six days after appeared under a Flag of Truce.

Capt. *Bean* the Interpreter was sent to meet them. They brought a Letter from *Winnenimmit* their Chief *Sagamore*, which was wrote in *French*. The import of which was to congratulate the *Gentlemens* Arrival on a design of *Peace*, which they earnestly desired to treat about, provided they might do it safely; being under some fear and jealousy. And indeed they had Cause of being so, for that about ten days before under a Flag of Truce, some of the *English* Treacherously attempted to lay violent Hands upon them, but lost one in the Skirmish, and had another wounded, which was the occasion of the like unhappy disaster that afterwards hapned unto Capt. *Saunders* in *Penobscot* Bay. They then moved, that in as much as many of their Men were scattered, (being out a hunting) that our Gentlemen would stay a little, which they consented to. And five days after, *Seven* came in under a Flag of Truce, making the usual signal; and informing the Commissioners they would wait on them to Mor-

Morrow; who after a friendly Entertainment were dismiss. The next day their whole Body came within a quarter of a Mile of the Garrison desiring the *English* to come to them; which they refused, saying, that they were sent from the several *Governments* to hear what they had to offer; but assured them that if they came to them no injury should be offered. After a short consultation they comply'd, provided that the *English* would engage it *in the Name of God*. And then they sent in thirteen of their *Chiefs*, expecting the like number of *English* to be sent them. So soon as they met, the Commissioners demanded what they had to offer, who complimented them with the great satisfaction they had in seeing them in so peaceable a disposition, and that it was also the intent and desire of their hearts. It was then ask'd wherefore they made War upon the *English*? Who replied, because of their Encroachments upon their Lands so far *Westward* as *Cape-Nawagen*, where two of their Men as they said were beaten to Death. Unto which 'twas answered, That that very Land was bought by the *English*, and that the Deeds from their Predecessours were ready to be shewn: And admitting it was true what they said, that the *English* did so inhumanly beat two of their *Indians*, yet it was not justifiable in them (according to the Articles of Peace) to commence a War at once, without first making Application to the *Government*, who at all times were ready to do them justice.

This Conference being over, they propos'd a further *Treaty*; which after some debate was resolved to be at *Boston*. They then moved for a
Cessation

Cessation of Arms, but our Commissioners, having no power, replied, that if they went to *Boston* it might probably be granted. But in the mean time moved that each Party should be on their Guard, for that it was the Custom of Nations to carry on the War on both sides till matters were fully concluded. The *Indians* reply'd that as they desired Peace, they were resolved on calling in their young Men, promising for themselves and those also of their *Tribe*, that no Hostility should be formed against us.

The Treaty being over, Capt *Loran* and *Ahanquid*, who were two of their Chiefs, accompanied our Gentlemen to *Boston*, where they were friendly Entertained, and after a Capitulation of matters, return'd in a Vessel prepared on purpose, with a promise of bringing more of their Chiefs with them in forty days after their arrival, for a final Issue of all differences.

Several Constructions and Censures were pass'd on this *Treaty*; some thinking the *English* were more forward for a Peace than the *Indians*, and that as we now knew their head quarters, might easily destroy their Corn, and distress them in their Fishery, which would bring them to a ready composition. Altho' the *Penobscot Indians* seem'd *Guarantee* for the other Tribes, yet as we knew them Treacherous, we could put no confidence in them, but rather lay our selves open unto a Snare, and become the more secure! Something like this accordingly fell out; for on *September* 15th a Party of them fell on some of *Cochecha* while at work in the Field, where they slew one, Scalpt another, cut off the Head of a third, and
carried

carried a fourth Captive; all which belong'd to the Family of the *Evans's*.

A few days after another Party attack'd a Garrison at *North Yarmouth*, but were so stoutly repulsed that they made no impression; but at their drawing off, kill'd several Cattel. Two days after some appear'd at *Mowsum* and then at *Damaru* Cove, which lies *Eastward* of *Kennebeck*, and is two Leagues within the line agreed upon; where they took and burnt two Shallops which belonged to *Stephen Hunuel*, and *Alexander Soaper*, whom with five Men and a Boy, they carried to the *Winniganse*, and knockt him on the head. Some conjectured these *Indians* came from *Canada*, others that they belong'd to the *Eastward*, for that an *English Jacket* was afterwards seen on one of them; but the *Eastern Indians* laid it on the other.

At the same time the *English* had several Companies out, as at *Amarascoggin*, *Rockamagug*, *Naridgwalk*, &c. Where Col. *Harmon* and others went, but made no discovery. Some thought that *We* hereby infring'd on the Articles made between them and us, unto which it may be replied, that these places were not within the *Penobscot* Line; and altho' they promis'd to do what they could in restraining others from falling on the *English*, yet as several Scouts from other Places were then out, they could not absolutely engage for them, Wherefore it was now requisite for us to secure our Frontiers.

About the 28th *September* 1725 Capt *Dwight* of Fort *Dummer* sent out a Scout of six Men *West*. who being upon their return sat down to Refresh them-

R

themselves; and hearing a noise like Runing, looked up, and saw fourteen *Indians* just upon them. Our Men fired at the Enemy, but were soon over powr'd by the *Indians*, who kill'd two, took three and one escaped.

The forty days before mentioned for coming in of the *Penobscot Indians*, with those of the other Tribes being near twice expired, gave great uneasiness for fear of some Mischief that was designed. But in the beginning of *November*, the several Captains hereafter mentioned came in, *viz. Sauguaaram,* alias *Sorun, Arexus, Francois Xavier, Megannumba,* where the following *Submission* and *Agreement* was concluded on.

The Submission and Agreement
Of the *Delegates* of the *Eastern* Indians.

WHEREAS the several Tribes of *Eastern* Indians, *viz.* The *Penobscot, Naridgwalk,* St. *John*'s, *Cape Sables,* and other *Tribes* inhabiting within his *Majesty*'s Territories of *New-England,* and *Nova-Scotia,* who have been engaged in the present War, from whom we *Sauguaaram,* alias *Sorun, Arexus, Francois-Xavier* and *Meganumbe,* are delegated and fully impowered to enter into Articles of Pacification with his Majesty's Governments of the *Massachusets-Bay, New-Hampshire* and *Nova-Scotia* ; HAVE contrary to the several Treaties they have solemnly entered into with the said Governments, made an open Rupture, and have continued some years in Acts of Hostility against the Subjects of his Majesty KING GEORGE

GEORGE within the said Governments; they being now sensible of the Miseries and Troubles they have involved themselves in, and being desirous to be restored to his Majesty's Grace and Favour, and to live in Peace with all his Majesty's Subjects of the said three Governments and the Province of *New-York* and Colony's of *Connecticut* and *Rhode-Island,* and that all former Acts of Injury be forgotten: HAVE concluded to make AND WE DO by these presents in the Name and Behalf of the said Tribes, MAKE our Submission unto His most Excellent Majesty GEORGE by the Grace of God of *Great Britain, France* and *Ireland,* King Defender of the Faith, *&c.* in as full and ample manner as any of our Predecessors have heretofore done.

AND WE DO hereby Promise and engage with the Honourable *WILLIAM DUMMER* Esq. As he is *Lieut. Governour* and Commander in Chief of his Majesty's Province of the *Massachusetts-Bay,* and with the Governours or Commanders in Chief of the said Province for the time being; That is to say,

WE the said Delegates for and in behalf of the several Tribes aforesaid, do promise and engage, That at all times for ever from and after the Date of these Presents, we and they will cease and forbear all Acts of *Hostility,* Injuries and Discord, towards all the Subjects of the Crown of *Great Britain,* and not offer the least Hurt, Violence, or Molestation to them or any of them in their Persons or Estates, but will henceforward hold and maintain a firm and constant Amity and Friendship with all the *English,* and will never con-

confederate or combine with any other Nation to their Prejudice.

THAT all the *Captives* taken in this prefent War fhall at or before the time of the further Ratification of this Treaty be reftored, without any Ranfom or Payment to be made for them or any of them.

THAT his Majefty's Subjects the *Englifh* fhall and may peaceably and quietly, enter upon, improve and for ever enjoy all and fingular their Rights of Land and former Settlements, Properties and Poffeffions, within the *Eaftern* parts of the faid Province of the *Maffachufets-Bay*; TOGETHER with all Iflands, Inlets, Shores, Beaches and Fifhery within the fame, without any Moleftation or Claimes by us or any other *Indians*, and be in no ways Molefted, interrupted or difturbed therein.

SAVING unto the *Penobfcot*, *Naridgwalk*, and other *Tribes* within his Majefty's *Province* aforefaid, and their natural Defcendants refpectively, all their Lands, Liberties and Properties not by them conveyed or fold to or poffeffed by any of the *Englifh* Subjects as aforefaid; As alfo the Priviledge of Fifhing, Hunting and Fowling as formerly.

THAT all Trade and Commerce which may hereafter be allowed betwixt the *Englifh* and the *Indians*, fhall be under fuch management and Regulation, as the Government of the *Maffachufets* Province fhall direct.

IF any Controverfy or Difference at any time hereafter happen to arife between any of the *Englifh* and *Indians*, for any real or fuppofed wrong

or

or injury done on either fide, no private Revenge shall be taken for the same, but proper Application shall be made to his Majesty's Government upon the place for Remedy or Redress thereof, in a due Course of Justice: We submiting our selves to be Ruled and Governed by his Majesty's Laws, and desiring to have the Benefit of the same.

WE also the said *Delegates* in behalf of the Tribes of *Indians* inhabiting within the *French* Teritories, (who have assisted us in this War) for whom we are fully impowered to Act in this present Treaty, Do hereby Promise and engage, that they and every of them shall henceforth cease and forbear all Acts of Hostility, Force, and Violence towards all and every, the Subjects of his Majesty the King of *Great Britain*.

WE do further in the behalf of the *Penobscot Indians* Promise and engage, that if any of the other Tribes intended to be included in this Treaty, shall notwithstanding refuse to confirm and Ratifie this present Treaty entred into on their behalf, and continue or renew Acts of Hostility against the *English*, in such Case the said *Penobscot* Tribe, shall joyn their Young Men with the *English* in reducing them to Reason.

IN the next place We the afore named *Delegates* Do Promise and engage with the Honourable *John Wentworth* Esq. as he is Lieut. Governour and Commander in Chief of his Majesty's Province of *New-Hampshire*, and with the Governours and Commanders in Chief of the said Province for the time being, That we and the Tribes we are deputed from, will henceforth cease and forbear

bear all Acts of Hostility, Injuries and Discords towards all the Subjects of his Majesty King *George* within the said *Province*; and we do understand and take it that the said Government of *New-Hampshire*, is also included and comprehended in all and every of the Articles aforegoing, excepting that Article respecting the regulating the Trade with us.

AND further, We the aforenamed *Delegates* Do Promise and engage with the Honourable *Laurence Armstrong* Esq Lieut. Governour and Commander in Chief of his *Majesty's* Province of *Nova-Scotia* or *Accadia*, to live in Peace with his Majesty's good Subjects and their Dependants in that Government, according to the Articles agreed on with Major *Paul Mascarene*, Commissioned for that purpose; And further to be Ratified as mentioned in the said Articles.

That this present *Treaty* shall be Accepted, Ratified and Confirmed, in a publick and solemn manner, by the Chiefs of the several *Eastern* Tribes of *Indians* included therein at *Falmouth* in *Casco-Bay*, some time in the Month of *May* next. In Testimony whereof we have Signed these Presents, and affixed our Seals.

Dated at the Council-Chamber in *Boston* in *New-England*, this fifteenth Day of *December*, Anno Dom. One Thousand Seven Hundred and Twenty Five. *Anno Regni Regis* Georgii Magnæ Britaniæ, *&c. Duodecimo.*

(127)

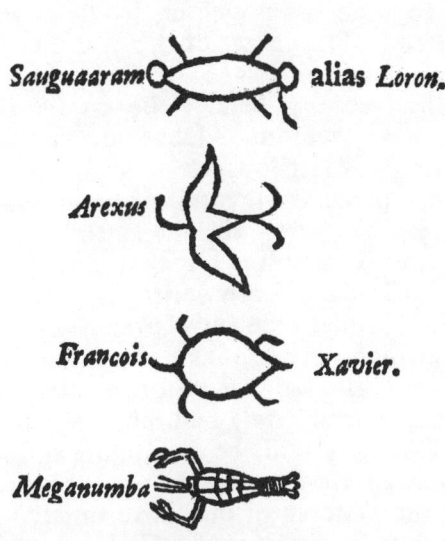

A True Copy taken from the Original, executed by the *Indian* Delegates before the General Assembly, *December* 15. 1725.

Atteft
    J. Willard, Secr.

Thus we have feen the Events of *twenty three* Years, in moſt of which we have heard nothing but the *ſound of the Trumpet, and the alarm of War*. And in the time of the intervening Peace, we met with many Interruptions and Acts of Hoſtility, which prevented the growth of our *Eaſtern* Settlements.

It's ſurprizing to think that ſo ſmall a number of *Indians* ſhould be able to diſtreſs a Country

try so large and populous, to the degree we have related. The *Charge* of the War in the last three Years was no less than *One hundred and seventy thousand pounds*; besides the constant Charge of watching, warding, scouting, making and repairing of Garrisons, *&c.* which may modestly be computed at upwards of *seventy thousand pounds* more. Yet after all, the Enemy have but little cause of Triumph; for that one third of them (at least) have been destroy'd, and one of their Tribes so shattered (at *Naridgwalk*) that they are never more like to make any formidable head.

Now as *Peace* seems once more to be concluded by the *Treaty* beforementioned, the greatest Difficulty will be to support and maintain it. If *Trading Houses*, which are now resolved on, (by the Wisdom of the Government) be well regulated, it may (under God) be a means of our Tranquility: Especially if the Government can also prevail with them to receive the *Ministry* for their instruction in the Principles of the true Religion.

But altho' it was agreed on with the several *Delegates* that the *Treaty* should be ratified and confirmed in a publick and solemn manner by the *Chiefs* of the several *Tribes* of the Eastern *Indians* at *Falmouth* in *Casco-Bay*, some time in the Month of *May*; yet when that time came they were not ready for it, but seem'd for some time uncertain and dilatory. Nevertheless the *Government* from time to time received Advices of their continued desires of Peace; and resolving that the failure should not be on our part, His *Honour the Lieutenant Governour* with a *Quorum of His Ma-*

Majesty's Council, and a number of *Gentlemen* of the House of *Representatives*; attended with a good *Guard*, and a fine train of *Young Gentlemen*, set out from *Boston* on *July* 14. and arrived at *Falmouth* the 16th.

On the 21*st*. His *Honour* received a Letter from *Wenemovet*, *Sagamore* and chief *Sachem* of the *Penobscot Tribe*, dated at St. *Georges* July 19. Praying him to meet the *Indians* at *Pemaquid*; which his Honour absolutely refused, requiring him to come to *Casco*, and promising him *safe conduct*.

On the 29th *Wenemovet* arrived, with a number of his Principal Men and others, about *forty*, and on the thirtieth the *Conference* for the *Ratification* of the late *Treaty* was enter'd on; and on the *sixth* of *August* it was concluded.

The *Penobscot Tribe* only appeared, but in behalf of all the *other* Tribes. The *Canada* Tribes had been sent to by them, and had sent a Letter (as they said) with two *Wampam Belts*; the one for their Brethren of *Penobscot*, in Token I suppose of their being concluded by them in the present *Treaty*, the other to be presented to our *Governour* upon the Ratification of the Treaty; which was accordingly presented.

The *Lieut. Governour* demanded of them, Why the *Narridgwalks* were not there? *Wenemovet* answered, that they had full power to act for them, and for the *Wowenocks* and the *Arreruguntenocks*, and the St. *Francois*.

The *Governments* had many and large *Conferences* with the *Indians*; worthy to be communicated to the Publick, and which would be an Entertainment to the Curious. In these *Conferences* the

Discre-

(130)

Discretion and Prudence of the *Salvages* was observable, as well as the Wisdom, Justice, Equity and Tenderness of the *Governours* on our part.

One of the first things that the *Indians* desired of our *Governours* was, That they would give order that the *Vessels* in the Harbour as well as the *Taverns* ashore might be restrained from selling any Liquors to their Young Men. The *Governour* told them, that he very much approved of that, and would give order accordingly.

On *Saturday*, July 30th when the Conference for the day was over, the *Lieut. Governour* told them, " To Morrow is the *Lords-Day*, on which we do no Business. *Loron*, their Speaker, answered readily, " To Morrow is our *Sabbath-Day*; we also keep the Day.

It may be a pleasure to the *Reader* to have the Words of the Ratification of the Treaty, both on *our* part and also on the part of the *Indians*.

On the *Indians* part it ran in the following Words.

WE the underwritten *Wenemovet*, chief *Sachem* and *Sagamore* of the *Penobscot Tribe*, and other the *Chiefs* with the rest of the said *Tribe* now convented, having had the within *Articles of Peace* distinctly and deliberately read over and interpreted to us ; Do by these Presents in a publick and solemn manner, as well for *ourselves* as for all the *within mentioned Tribes*, from whom we are delegated and fully impowered, *Ratify*, *Affirm* and *Confirm* all and singular the within Articles of Peace, *To His most Sacred Majesty King GEORGE*: And that the same and each of them be, and
shall

shall continue and remain in full force, efficacy and power, to all Intents and Purposes whatsoever.

Done and Concluded at *Falmouth* in *Casco-Bay* before his Honour *William Dummer* Esq. Lieut. Governour and Commander in chief of his *Majesty's Province* of the *Massachusets Bay* in *New-England*, and his *Majesty's Council* of *said Province*: The Honourable *John Wentworth* Esq. Lieut. Governnour of his *Majesty's Province of New-Hampshire*, and several of his Majesty's *Council* of said *Province*: And Major *Paul Mascarene*, delegated from his *Majesty's* Province of *Nova Scotia* or *L' Accadia*; and the several *Gentlemen* that subscribe hereto.

Witness our hands and Seals the *fifth day of August* in the *thirteenth* year of the *Reign* of our Sovereign Lord GEORGE, by the Grace of God of *Great Britain France* and *Ireland*, King, Defender of the Faith, &c. Annoq. Dom. 1726.

On *our* part the *Ratification* of the Treaty ran thus.

By the Honourable *William Dummer* Esq. Lieut. Governour and Commander in Chief of his *Majesty's Province of the Massachusetts-Bay in New England*.

Whereas *Wenemovet* the chief *Sachem of Penobscot*, with others his *Chiefs* and the rest of said *Tribe*, Convented at *Casco-Bay* the 5th day of *August* 1726. Having solemnly and publickly Ratified

tified the *Treaty of Submission* made at *Boston* the 15th day of *December* last, and delivered the same to me, which I have according accepted;

I do hereby *Ratify and Confirm* all the *Articles* in the within mentioned *Instrument*.

Given under my Hand and Seal at Arms at *Falmouth* in *Casco-Bay*, the sixth day of *August*, in the thirteenth year of the Reign of our Sovereign Lord King GEORGE, by the Grace of God of *Great Britain*, &c. Annoq. Dom. 1726.

WILLIAM DUMMER.

By the Command of his
  Honour the Lieut.
Governour,

John Wainwright,
Clerk of the Council.

After the Ratification was over the *Lieut. Governour* among other things, desired them to say, what Measures they purpos'd to take, whereby the Inhabitants on our Frontiers may be made easie and safe, notwithstanding the *Narridgwalks* &c. who did not personally appear to Ratify the Articles of the present *Treaty*?

They answered, That they would have the Inhabitants of the Frontiers to be very *careful*; and that as soon as they return'd home it should be their first care to send to all the *Tribes*, and let them know that there is a Peace made.

The *Lieut. Governour* ask'd them, Will you lay your Commands and Injunctions on the other Tribes for that purpose, as far as you are able? *Loron* answered, We will do our utmost to oblige 'em to live peaceably towards us.

The *Lieut. Governour* replied, Do you say you will *resent* it, if any hostile Acts or Injuries should be committed against our People?

Loron. We will *resent* such Actions, and joyn our young Men with yours in such a case, and oblige them to be quiet and sit down. We mean in case any of the *Tribes* should rise against us, or resist us, we will take effectual means to set 'em down by force. As to the *first Treaty* we reckoned our selves obliged to this, but we account we are under much more and stronger Obligations to it now; since the Engagements onr whole *Tribe* have taken upon them, in *ratifying* the Articles of the *Treaty*. We shall take effectual care therefore that any such Persons be obliged to sit down.

We have given our Words, and repeated our Promises and Engagements; and our Words are written down, and they will appear afterwards against us.

When the whole Conference was transcribed, it was on *August* 11. (may the *Day* be memorable and happy to us and ours after us) distinctly read over and interpreted to *Wenemovet* and the Indians with him; and the *Lieut. Governour* ask'd them if they understood it, and whether it was rightly taken down? They answered, That the Conference was rightly taken down, and not a word missing in it.

His

His *Honour* then for their more full Satisfaction subscribed his Name to it, and then delivered it to *Wenemovet*, chief *Sachem*, who with his principal Men subscrib'd to it, and deliver'd it back to his *Honour*.

And thus we hope, by the Will of God, that a happy Foundation is laid for a lasting Peace. And we cannot conclude without a thankful Acknowlegement of the great favour and mercy of God to us, in the wise Conduct given unto His Honour the *Lieut. Governour*, both in the management of the *War*, and also of the *Treaty of Peace*. May the Comforts and Rewards of a *faithful Administration* remain to Him for ever; and the happy Fruits of *Peace* unto these *Provinces*.

F I N I S.

Advertisement.

IN Page 102. there is a great omission, which the *Reader* is desired to correct, *viz.* In the Article relating to Lieut. *Bean* and Company, at the bottom of the Page, it should have been added, One of their principal *Indians* was kill'd, and his Scalp brought to *Boston*, for which said *Bean* and Company receiv'd an *hundred pounds*.

Notes

The foot-notes supplied by the Publishing Committee in their reprint of Penhallow's *Indian Wars* (*Collections of the New Hampshire Historical Society*, I, 1824.) are here indicated: [N. H.]. Other notes found in the Cincinnati reprint of 1859, are indicated: [C.]. Unsigned notes are those of the editor. Widely varying statements, phraseology and spelling, in the original manuscript in the Library of Congress are indicated: [MS.]. For the authorities quoted in these notes see the appended Bibliography.

Page iii.
Line 13.—Cotton Mather. "Decennium Luctuosum. | An | History | of | Remarkable Occurrences, | In the Long | War, | which | New-England hath had with the | Indian Salvages, | From the year 1688. | to the Year 1698. | Faithfully Composed and Improved." Pp. 254, (1). 8vo, B. Green and J. Allen, for Samuel Phillips. [Boston]. 1699. It includes a Sermon, at Boston-Lecture, 27 d, 7 m. 1698, on "the great Calamities of a War with Indian Salvages." This has long been extremely rare. See Brinley *Catalogue*, No. 1097.

Page vi.
Line 16.—Pray. This anecdote has been often repeated but rarely given as Penhallow's personal experience. See: Whiton, p. 65; Barstow, p. 126.

Page 1.
The border pieces at the top of this page and on page 135, are forms in common use in the 17th and 18th centuries. Judge Samuel Sewall's book label for example bore similar but slightly larger border-pieces, with an interrogation

point, as here, to make out the measure. This use of punctuation characters was considered no blemish in the composition of these ornaments.

Page 2.

Line 17.—Joseph Dudley, [1647–1720], Governor of Mass., Maine, and N. H., and Thomas Povey, Lt.-Gov., arrived at Boston, June 11, 1702. Williamson, p. 34. **Line 23.**—Penhallow himself attended this Congress at Casco. **Line 25.**—Our author makes little effort at consistency in the spelling of Indian names nor does the compositor seriously attempt to follow his copy. The results achieved in attempting to represent sounds heard so differently by different men are interesting. There are some ninety different spellings of the Confederation name "Abnaki," and more than thirty spellings of "Pigwacket." See note for line 12, page 40. **Line 28.**—Pigwackett in manuscript—a case in point of above. Bouton ascribes the form "Pequackett" to Penhallow, which is neither his written nor printed form. **Line 30.**—240 men. [MS.].

Page 4.

Line 23.—"double shotted." [MS.]. **Line 29.**—"not affect one without the other." [MS.]. Williamson quotes much from Penhallow here, and apparently from a copy of this original edition, as shown by the pagination in his references. Few writers seem to have had access to a copy of the original edition.

Page 5.

Line 10.—In the year 1703. [N. H.]. **Line 16.**—The Indians took and killed 130 people. Belknap, I, 264. [N. H.]. **Line 28.**—See Baker, p. 47. **Line 29.**—See Bourne, p. 246. **Line 31.**—Arundel in 1718; Kennebunkport in 1821. The cape was named by Capt. John Smith in 1614. The term *Porcus Piscis*, Hog-fish, has had a dozen accepted spellings in English. Penhallow uses three forms in his manuscript: Porposs, Porpos and Porpas. The town was incorporated in 1653 as Cape Porpus; it is Porpoise in Records of 1672.

Page 6.

Line 5.—Spurwink is the settlement near Richmond's island in Maine. It was the seat of Robert Trelawney who early came over, and had a grant of nearly all the lands in Cape Elizabeth, and of the lands on the neck of Casco, and extending some way into the country. [N. H.]. **Line 10.** —"sent Eliza Scammon with a flag of truce, but the officer, well knowing their intrigues, slighted the message, secured the captive, and suffered none to approach than what the muzzle of his guns gave licence for; however, by a long siege, they were so reduced, that were it not for supplys sent them from New Hampshire they had totally been overthrown." [MS.]. **Line 17.**—Perpooduck is the point directly opposite Portland. Greenleaf's *Eccl. Hist.* p. 87. [N. H.]. **Line 26.**—Quis talio fando—Temperet a Lachrymis. [MS.]. **Line 27.**—Casco was what was anciently called Falmouth. Sullivan, p. 213. [N. H.]. **Line 28—** Major John March. **Line 30.**—Messacombuit. [MS.]. Moxus. Williamson, p. 43.

Page 7.

Line 19.—Phippen, Abbott, p. 263. Phippenny, Williamson.

Page 8.

Line 3.—Bobassin, Abbott, p. 263. **Line 11.**—Cyprian Southack, Drake's *French and Indian Wars*, p. 281. Southwick, Williamson, p. 44. **Line 14.**—August 17, 1703. [N. H.]. **Line 16.**—Widow Mary Hussey (?), Coolidge and Mansfield, p. 513. "who was generally lamented by that sect," erased in the Manuscript. **Line 21.**—On the 8th October 1703, Zebediah Williams and John Nims, were taken prisoners at Deerfield, and carried to Canada. Williams died there; Nims, with some others, made his escape and returned to Deerfield in 1705. [N. H.].

Page 9.

Line 5.—Hunnewell, Williamson. But see the exploit of Richard Hunnewell, possibly a descendant, in Coolidge and Mansfield, p. 296. **Line 6.**—Blackpoint, not in manuscript. Black Point was one part of Scarborough, Me. [N. H.]. **Line 13.**—Wyatt, Williamson. **Line 15.**—........ time but the later, having stayd his cruze, was obligd to return; and left Wells behind, expecting that he would stay and defend them, but being timerous, did rather dispirit than animate the besieged, and tooke ym on board with

NOTES.

their familys, which the Enemy observing soon after set it on fire. [MS.]. **Line 21.**—Bragdon's. [MS.]. **Line 22.** —Hannah Parsons, Williamson. Widow of William Parsons. **Line 24.**—The word is differently spelled. Winthrop has it Pegwaggett; Sullivan, Peckwalket and Pickwocket; Belknap, Pigwacket. The true orthography is said to be Pequawkett. [N. H.]. **Line 34.**—The success of Colonel March encouraged the government to offer a bounty of 40 Pounds for scalps. Belknap, I, p. 265. [N.H.].

Page 10.

Line 2.—Salmon Falls. [MS.]. Scarce a week but some damage or other was done: At Salmon-Falls five soldiers carelesly walking from ye Fort were ambusht; [MS.]. **Line 12.**—William Tyng was born April 22, 1679, promoted Major, 1709. He was wounded at Chelmsford, dying at Concord a few days later, in the summer of 1710. So says Penhallow, p. 59, and Wilkes Allen, *History of Chelmsford,* giving the date as 1711 (Green, *Groton during the Indian Wars*), is probably wrong. He was a son of Col. Jonathan Tyng (Williamson says of Edward Tyng) commanding Dunstable (then Massachusetts) forces, who single handed and alone defended his settlement during the Indian War in 1675. William Tyng commanded as Lieutenant the forces of fortified houses in Dunstable in 1703, but was promoted to a Captaincy in charge of a Massachusetts company of "snow-shoe men." For the record of payment of the company for this service, from Dec. 28 to Jan. 25, 1703-04, *Mass. Council Records*, Vol. IV, p. 10. **Line 17.**—"Stephens, of Andover, but neither had ye like success." [MS.]. **Line 19.**—Capt. John Gilman of Exeter, Capt. Chesley and Capt. Davis of Oyster river, marched with their companies on snow shoes into the woods; but returned without success. Belknap, I, 266. [N. H.]. **Line 26.**—"Capt. Brown that some dropt their blanketts, others their arrows sleds and knapsacks leaving nine of their dead behind, besides several who were wounded, wch. so enraged them yt. at their return they Executed their revenge on Joseph Ring (a captive then among them) wm. they fastened to a stake and burnt alive with loud huzzas and acclamations of joy being never better pleased than when their

NOTES.

ears are filled with the solemn cries of such dying persons.
[MS.]. **Line 33.**—Joseph Bradberry's. [MS.]. **Line 34.**
—Haverhill. [MS.].

Page 11.

Line 30.—the most northerly settlement of Connecticut
River. [MS.].

Page 12.

Line 1.—others by reason of a letter from one of Westfield, who sojourning that Winter at Albany and loath his wife should bee under fire, signifyed, that altho there was such advice, yet but few took notice of it; However, [MS.]. **Line 10.**—Indians. "and the Evening before, a black cloud was seen at Hatfield, which on a sudden was turned as red as blood; In ye morning" [MS.]. February 29, 1704. **Line 16.**—40 of ym attackt the Fort. [MS.]. **Line 18.**—"about" for "above." [MS.]. **Line 20.**—Artel or Hertel. Francis Hertel de Rouville, 1643-1722. **Line 24.**—Rev. John Williams was son of Stephen Williams, Esq. of Roxbury, where he was born Dec. 10, 1664; graduated at Harvard College 1683; ordained the first minister in Deerfield, May 1686; captured by the Indians, Feb. 29, 1704; returned from captivity and arrived at Boston, Nov. 21, 1706; died June 12, 1729. He published a narrative of his captivity and sufferings entitled "The Redeemed Captive returning to Zion," which in 1775, had passed through six editions. [N. H.]. **Line 26.**—"whereof ten were stifled." [MS.]. **Line 27.**—The names of those persons who were killed and taken captive at Deerfield at this time, are preserved in Rev. Mr. Williams' *Redeemed Captive. Appendix.* [N. H.]. **Line 30.**—"lest by pittying one another they became greater objects of pitty ymselves. The Enemy after this divided into severall parties; some Engagd in plundring; others in burning and destroying what Ever they could, In so much that day and night was wholy spent in such tragical actions. The morning"............ [MS.].

Page 13.

Line 28.—Men from Port Royal. [MS.]. **Line 34.**—Plymouth Shore. [MS.].

Page 14.

Line 2.—Virginey. [MS.]. **Line 4.**—25 officers. [MS.].

Line 17.—"Majr. Mason from Connecticut with 95 of the Pequod and Mohegan Indians were posted at Newchewanock, who were very terrified" [MS.]. **Line 22.**—Meader. [MS.]. Meadear, Williamson. **Line 22.**—Edward Taylor nere a saw mill near Lampreyeal River.[MS.].

Page 15.

Line 3.—Bourne, p. 259, gives names. **Line 9.**—Possummuck. [MS.]. Now a part of East-Hampton, Massachusetts. [N. H.]. **Line 31.**—Major Whiting, [MS.].

Page 16.

Lines 10-12.—Not in manuscript. **Line 17.**—Benjamin Church, now a Colonel. **Line 27.**—The names of the officers under Col. Church, as given in his memoirs of the expedition, were Lt. Col. John Gorham, Major Winthrop Hilton, Captains John Brown, James Cole, John Cook, Isaac Mirick, John Harradon, Constant Church, John Dyer, Joshua Lamb, Caleb Williamson, and Edward Church. [N. H.].

Page 17.

Line 1.—May 25th. [MS.]. **Line 3.**—Le-febure. [MS.]. Church, *Indian Wars*, calls him Lafaure. **Line 14.**—In the *New Hampshire Collections* (I, p. 33), this name is misprinted "D. Young." **Line 18.**—Castine's daughter and several children. Abbott, p. 368. "Passamaquado." [MS.]. **Line 19.**—D'Sart. [MS.]. **Line 24.**—Lotriel. [MS.]. Benjamin Church found "Mr. Lateril" in these parts, "a-trading with the Indians" in 1696. **Line 25.**—Gourdon. [MS.]. Benjamin Church in his report to Gov. Dudley mentions the capture of Gourdan only. Thomas Church, *Indian Wars*, says "finding that Madam Sharkee had left her silk clothes and fine linen behind her, our forces were desirous to have pursued and taken her. But Colonel Church forbade," etc. Sharkee undoubtedly was not taken. Drake (Church, *Fr. and Ind. Wars*, p. 260) thinks Penhallow was mistaken about the capture of Sharkee; he escaped with his wife into the woods. **Line 34.**—Menis. [MS.]. Minas, Williamson. Belknap, I, p. 334, says that they destroyed the towns of Minas and Chiegnecto, which Penhallow spells (p. 43) Sachenecto.

NOTES.

Page 18.

Line 3.—The following is in the manuscript between "Surrender" and "Their Answer." "Wee declare to you the many Cruelties and barbarities which you and the Indians have been guilty off, towards us, in laying wast our Country from the East of Casco, and the places adjacent, particularly the horrid action at Deerfield the last winter, in killing and massacring, murdering, and seassing, without giving any notice, or opportunity to ask quarters at yr. hand, and after all, carrying the remainder into captivity in the height of winter (of which they killd many in the journey, and exposed ye rest unto the hardship of cold and famine, wors than death itself, wch cruelties we are every day exposd unto, and exercisd with. Wee also declare that as wee have made some beginnings of killing and seaszing (which wee have not been wont to doe or allow) that wee are now come with a great number of English and Indians (all volunteers) with a resolution to subdue aed make sensible of your cruelties to us, by treating you after ye same maner. In the last place we declare, that in as much as some of you have shewn kindness to our Captives, and Expressd a desire of bying under the English Government, that upon laying down your arms wee will give you good quarter, but if you refuse, may expect that we will treat you with the utmost severity.
June 24, 1704.

      Benjn. Church,
      John Goreham, Lt. Col.,
      Winthrop Hilton, Majr.

To the Chiefe Comander of the
 Town of Minis and the Inhabitants thereof.

The way to Minis (unless in time of flood) being almost impassible, prevented their going so soon as otherwise they would; but the answer," etc. . . . . . . [MS.]. **Line 15.**—"Casks, and staving ym. to pieces; and being resolved to pursue them, Capt. Cook and Capt. Church were ordered to lead the two wings, and Lieut. Baker to fall in the centre, who not so carefull as he might be, was shot, with another by him; which were the only two that fell at this time and not above six in the whole expedition"; [MS.]. But Baker was probably Lieutenant Barker, and the "one more" was J. Briggs. **Line 27.**—Port Royal in which were only five houses standing out of sight of the Fort. [MS.].

Page 19.

Line 5.—See Bourne, Williamson and Church. **Line 17.**—a Frenchman. [MS.]. **Line 27.**—See continuation in Bourne, p. 261. **Line 32.**—Belknap, I, p. 334, says Tasker.

Page 20.

Line 8.—Lymon. [MS.]. **Line 11.**—Kill'd by himself with one Englishman and five Maheggan Indians. [MS.]. The "Account," three printed pages here, is not found in the manuscript. It may have been inserted by Dr. Colman.

Page 23.

Line 9.—May 11, 1704, John Allen and his wife were killed at, or near Deerfield. Sergeant Hasks was wounded about the same time, but escaped to Hatfield. [N. H.] **Line 20.**—"Advice from Albany; Yet two friend Indians were kill'd [MS.]. **Line 23.**—"coming 30 miles off, which did put the country into so great a consternation," etc. [MS.]. There are many minor variations between the manuscript and the printed text on this page. **Line 25.**—"On the second of August, Major Whiting," etc. [MS.].

Page 24.

Line 10.—Enterprise, not willing to adventure either on Hatfield or North-Hampton. [MS.]. **Line 13.**—July 19, 1702, Thomas Russell of Deerfield was killed. [N. H.]. The Indians commenced their attack on Lancaster on the 31st July, early in the morning. In their first onset they killed Lieut. Nathaniel Wilder, near the gate of his garrison; and on the same day, three others, viz. Abraham How, John Spaulding and Benjamin Hutchins, near the same Garrison. Rev. Mr. Harrington's *Century Sermon.* [N. H.]. In this sermon of Rev. Timothy Harrington, published in Boston (1753) the inaccuracies of our author are noticed—"Some of the Accounts which Mr Penhallow

NOTES.

hath given of the Mischiefs done in this town by the Enemy, are in diverse Cases not only imperfect, but very Erroneous, which are doubtless owing to the wrong Information he had." **Line 14.**—Tyng. [MS.]. **Line 26.** —Quabaug, now Brookfield. [N. H.]. **Line 34.**—Nashway. [MS.].

Page 25.

Line 1.—Wylder. [MS.]. **Line 3.**—"bury" for "carry off." [MS.]. **Line 6,**—On the 8th of August, 1704, as several persons were busy in spreading flax, on a plain, about eighty rods from the house of Mr. Thomas Rice, and a number of boys with them, a number of Indians, seven or ten, suddenly rushed down a woody hill near by, and knocked on the head Nahor Rice, the youngest boy, and seized Asher and Adonijah, sons of Mr. Thomas Rice, and two others, Silas and Timothy, sons of Mr. Edmund Rice, and carried them away to Canada. The persons engaged in spreading flax, escaped safely to the house. Asher in about four years, returned, being redeemed by his father. His brother, Adonijah, grew up in Canada, and married there. Silas and Timothy mixed with the Indians; lost their mother tongue, had Indian wives, and children by them; and lived at Cagnawaga. The last became the third of the six Chiefs of the Cagnawagas, and was known among them by the name of Oughtsorongoughton. See Whitney's *History of Worcester*, pp. 121-123. [N. H.]. **Line 7.**—Amesberry, Haverhill. [MS.]. **Line 12.**—Asting. [MS.]. **Line 15.**—Kill'd the Sentinel and put ye rest to flight. [MS.[. **Line 17.**—The N. H. reprint modernizes the spelling. **Line 21.**—Leveret. [MS.]. **Line 22.**—Livingstone. [MS.]. **Line 23.**—"were appointed Agents to negotiate that affair; whose conduct was such as gained a good esteem and reception among them; and of fixing a firm allegance to the Brittish Crown; that altho the French had used severall means wherby to pervert them; yet were resolved the reject their offers, and as a testimony thereof, did promise to take up the hatchet." [MS.].

Page 26.

Line 15.—Bonavist. [MS.]. **Line 18.**—Guill. [MS.].

NOTES.

Page 27.

Line 21.—This "one" was Samuel Prescott, according to a manuscript note in one of the surviving copies of the book. **Line 23.**—"through a trap door into ye flanker." [MS.].

Page 28.

Line 8.—Norridgewock. This name has been subject to as many methods of spelling as its neighbor, Androscoggin. It was a celebrated ancient Indian town, on the Kennebeck River, about eighty-four miles from its mouth, by the course of the river. Sullivan, p. 31-32. [C.]. **Line 18.**—Partrick. [MS.]. **Line 34.**—Port-rosua. [MS.]. Probably Port-Roseway. [N. H.].

Page 29.

Line 6.—Samuel Hill. **Line 8.**—Philippe de Rigaud, Marquis de Vaudreuil, (1640-1725) Governor of Canada, the ancestor of a long line of eminent French officers. His early printed signature appears as Veaudreuil. **Line 17.**—"to Canada, accompanied by Capt. Courtemarch" [MS.].

Page 30.

Line 7.—Supercoss. [MS.]. Daniel de'Auger de Subercase. Jeremiah Dummer wrote, (*A Letter to a Noble Lord, concerning the Late Expedition to Canada*, London, 1712), "In the year 1704-5, Monsieur Subercass marched from Placentia at the head of 600 man (most of 'em Canadians) and besieg'd Fort William in New-Foundland for five weeks.". . . . "The enemy burnt St. John's; the loss was 80,000 Pounds." The loss from the second attack, in 1705, according to Dummer, was 150,000 Pounds, not reckoning 48 pieces of cannon, ammunition and stores. But on the authority of Charlevoix there were but 450 men, not 550. **Line 33.**—Samuel Moody of Falmouth.

Page 31.

Line 8.—Killed five, says Drake. **Line 12.**—Bonavist. [MS.]. **Line 21.**—"in Kittery" not in manuscript. **Line 23.**—Mrs. Holt, and she was captured only, according to Abbott, p. 273. **Line 29.**—Eastward, in the manuscript. **Line 32.**—Crepo. [MS.].

NOTES.

Page 32.

Line 7.—York. "Reddick," for Neddick, in manuscript. **Line 13.**—"A little boy, with awful torture." Abbott, p. 373. **Line 14.**—On the same day, Thomas Sawyer and his son Elias Sawyer, and John Bigle were taken captive from Lancaster. Harrington's *Century Sermon.* [N. H.]. **Line 32.**—Wheeler, wife and two children killed; four sons escaped by hiding in a cave. Belknap, I, 339. **Line 34.**—Shapley. Abbott.

Page 33.

Line 6.—A favorite method of torture, says Abbott. **Line 11.**—"Inhabitants," for "Government." [MS.]. **Line 15.**—Payne. [MS.]. **Line 18.**—Ferret. [MS.]. **Lines 24-25.**—Not in manuscript. **Line 27.**—Rows. See: Drake, *French and Indian Wars.*

Page 34.

Line 18.—"seized, and t'was vehemently suspected, that some of figure and distinction (who stood behind ye Curtain) were secret Actor therein, for they did what they could to Extenuate the crime & to get the Indictment altered from that of Treason unto high misdemeanor; . . . . fees; but what the Event was, on one, and the other, I refer to ye publick Records, wch make mention ym." [MS.].

Page 35.

Line 2.—They had been ranging the woods in the vicinity, and came towards night to this garrison; apprehending no danger, turned their horses loose upon the interval, piled their arms and harness in the house, and began a carousal, to exhilarate their spirits after the fatigues of the day. A party of Indians had lately arrived in the vicinity, and on that day had designed to attack both Wells' and Galusha's garrisons. One of their number had been stationed to watch each of these houses, to see that no assistance approached, and no alarm was given. A short time previous to the approach of the cavalry, the Indian stationed at Wells' had retired to his party, and reported that all was safe. At sunset, a Mr. Cumings and his wife went out to milk their cows, and left the gate open. The Indians, who had advanced undiscovered, started up, shot Mrs. Cumings dead upon the spot, and wounded her husband. They then rushed through the open gate into the house, with all the horrid yells of conquering savages, but stared with amazement on finding the room filled with soldiers merrily feasting. Both parties were completely amazed, and neither acted with much propriety. The soldiers, so suddenly interrupted in their jovial entertainment, found themselves called to fight, when entirely destitute of arms, and incapable of obtaining them. The greater part were panic-struck, and unable to fight or fly. Fortunately, all were not in this sad condition; some six or seven courageous souls, with chairs, clubs, and whatever they could seize upon, furiously attacked the advancing foe. The Indians who were as much surprised as the soldiers, had but little more courage than they, and immediately took to their heels for safety; thus yielding the house, defeated by one quarter their number of unarmed men. The trumpeter, who was in the upper part of the house at the commencement of the attack, seized his trumpet and began sounding an alarm, when he was shot dead by an Indian on the stair-way. He was the only one of the party killed.

The savages disappointed in this part of their plan, immediately proceeded to Galusha's, two miles distant; took possession of, and burnt it. One woman only escaped. Had the company at Wells' armed and immediately pursued, they might probably have prevented this disaster; but they spent so much time in arming and getting their horses that the enemy had an opportunity to perpetrate the mischief and escape uninjured.

The woman above mentioned, when the Indians attacked the house, sought refuge in the cellar, and concealed herself under a dry cask. After hastily plundering the house, and murdering, as they supposed, all who were in it, the Indians set it on fire and immediately retired. The woman in this critical situation, attempted to escape by the window, but found it too small; she however, succeeded in loosening the stones till she had opened a hole sufficient to admit of her passage, and with the house in flames over her head, she forced herself out, and crawled into the bushes, not daring to rise for fear she would be discovered. In the

NOTES.

bushes she lay concealed until the next day, when she reached one of the neighboring garrisons.

Cumings, at Wells' garrison, had his arm broken, but was so fortunate as to reach the woods while the Indians were engaged in the house. That night he lay in a swamp in the northerly part of what at present constitutes the town of Tyngsborough, about one quarter of a mile west of the great road as it now runs, and a few rods south of the state line. The next day he arrived at the garrison near the residence of the late Col. Tyng.—Farmer & Moore's *Collections*, II, pp. 303, 304. [N. H.]. This Mrs. Cumings has been identified as Elizabeth Kinsley, wife of John Cumings. See: *Granite State Magazine*, I, p. 145. **Line 5.**—Galucia's. Farmer & Moore's *Collections*, II, 303. The N. H. reprint reads: Galusha. **Line 20.**—House. Wells' garrison, which was in the southerly part of Dunstable, N. H., about half a mile from the state line, near James Baldwin's house, on a place known by the name of the Blanchard Farm, east of the great road to Boston. Galusha's, was about two miles south-west of this, on Salmon brook, at a place formerly called Glasgow, on which Henry Turrell now lives. [N. H.]

Page 36.

Line 3.—Jo English, as he was called, was much distinguished for his attachment to the white inhabitants. In a preceding war with the Indians, he had been taken a prisoner from the vicinity of Dunstable and carried to Canada, from whence by his shrewdness and sagacity, he effected his escape, with one English captive, and returned to his friends in Dunstable. The Indians had for a long time endeavored to retake him, and he was peculiarly obnoxious to them; and at the time above mentioned, while he was accompanying Capt. Butterfield and his wife on a visit to their friends, they pursued him, and just as he was upon the point of gaining a thicket, they shot him through the thigh, which brought him to the ground, and they afterwards dispatched him with their tomahawks. [N. H.]. **Line 26.**—"July 23" [MS.]. See: Green, *Sketch of Groton*, p. 47-48. July 21, 1706. Dr. Samuel A. Green, with his habitual care, cleared up the matter of the names of these soldiers. Two were brothers, Ebenezer Seger, killed, and Henry Seger, Jr., taken prisoner, probably. The third was Nathaniel Healey. They were "all new-Cambridge (Newton) men." See Rev. John Pike's *Journal*, *Pro. Mass. Hist. Soc.*, for Sept. 1875.

Page 37.

Line 10.—Mr. Sheldon (that faithful Agent) was once more perswaded to go to Canada . . . . . . but was prevented by the treachery of the Jesuits. [MS.].

Page 38.

Line 4.—A favorite story of Indian cruelty, many times quoted; no one seems to have noticed the obvious typographical error *back* for *bank*. See: facsimile page of manuscript. **Line 10.**—Hoise. Old form—found in Swift, Hakluyt, the King James' version, etc. **Line 19.**—Mrs. Hannah Parsons, wife of William Parsons.

Page 39.

Line 27.—"Head" for "scalp." [MS.]

Page 40.

Line 10.—Nathaniel Tibbitts, and on ye 21st they shot at Capt. Larabie as he came down Saco River. [MS.] **Line 12.**—Assacombuit. [MS.]. De la Potherie calls him Pierre Jeanbeovilh, the compositor having made the first letters into Pierre Jean, for "Nescam," and in despair beovilh for "biouit." He was wounded at Haverhill in 1708, where he fought with his French sabre. Shea, quoting this passage of Penhallow, adds, "Whence Penhallow derived this, we know not. Prejudice, here as elsewhere, probably supplied ideas which he gives as facts". A contemporary newspaper says that he died in June, 1727. He was an important Abnaki Chief. See: Charlevoix's *History of New France*, (N. Y., 1900.)

Page 41.

Line 24.—One of several passages in the book manifesting the credulity of some early New Englanders. See also, pp. 16 and 116. For "ninety miles", the manuscript reads "thirty leagues".

Page 42.

Line 1.—Wainwright. [MS.] **Line 7.**—Deptford. [MS.]

NOTES. 15

Line 9.—Hull. [MS.]. The date should be May 13, not March 13, 1707; See: Holmes *Annals,* I, 497, and Charlevoix.

Page 43.

Line 7.—"Yet to give him......Shoulders to bear", not in the manuscript. **Line 22.**—The N. H. reprint gives Chignecto. **Line 26.**—"Secured their lines, the bombs flying to such a degree." [MS.]. **Line 33.**—Fort-Major. [MS.] The descent on Port Royal cost Massachusetts more than 22,000 Pounds and about 30 lives.

Page 44.

Line 4.—Philip Carpenter. [MS.] **Line 7.**—Summersbee. [MS.] **Line 14.**—"before he could get clear one made towards him with his advanced hatchet, which he perceiving, presented his pistoll, and caused him to withdraw by which means he made his Escape" (and other small differences). [MS.] Stephen Gilman was taken and killed finally, at Kingston in 1712. Coolidge and Mansfield, p. 545. **Line 18.**—July 16, 1707, Mr. Jonathan White, of Lancaster, was killed by the Indians. Harrington. [N. H.]. **Line 34.**—This was Jonathan Wilder. [N. H.].

Page 45.

Line 1.—On the 18th of August, 1707, as two women in Northborough, Ms., were out a short distance from the fort gathering herbs, the Indians discovered and pursued them. One Mrs. Mary Fay got safe into the fort; the other Mary Goodenow, a young and unmarried woman, was taken and carried over the brook into the edge of Marlborough, and there, a little south of the great road, and nigh to Sandy Hill, she was killed and scalped. The enemy were pursued and overtaken in what is now Sterling, where an obstinate engagement took place, in which John Farrar and Richard Singletary, were killed. The Indians at length fled, leaving some plunder and some of their packs, in one of which the scalp of Mary Goodenow was found. See: Whitney's *Hist. of Worcester,* p. 274. [N. H.]. **Line 3.**—Henry Elkins, Sept. 15, 1707. [N. H.]. **Line 23.**—View either of besetting York or Wells for at Winter-Harbour on September 21st. with one hundred and forty, etc. [MS.]. **Line 26.**—At Anchor, and lashed together. [MS.]. **Line 30.**—Near, 30 yards. [MS.].

Page 46.

Line 29.—The Indians lost 30 killed and wounded. Abbott, p. 276. **Line 30.**—Newchewanock. [MS.].

Page 47.

Line 6.—Josiah Littlefield. For a long account of Littlefield, see Bourne, p. 267. **Line 13.**—"design against us, but twas not known, where they would make their first Onsett; upon which severall frontier Towns were strenthened; but on some misunderstanding or other, among ymselves, not above 150 came; who on the 29th of August," etc. [MS.]. **Line 33.**—Rev. Benjamin Rolfe graduated at Harvard College, 1684; was ordained in Haverhill, in January, 1694. Saltonstall's *Hist. Haverhill.* [N. H.]. **Line 34.**—October 26, 1708, E. Field was killed in Deerfield. [N. H.].

Page 48.

Line 1.—Hayes of Simsberry. [MS.]. **Line 10.**—Mehaman Hinsdell. [MS.]. **Line 12.**—Belknap, says May 5th. **Line 15.**—Moodey. [MS.]. **Line 17.**—Soon after, Bartholomew Stephenson was killed at Oyster River. In May, this year, Lieut. John Wells and John Burt were lost, in a skirmish with the enemy. They belonged to Deerfield. *Appendix* to Williams' *Narrative.* [N.H.]. **Line 18.**—North Hampton, with seaven English. [MS.]. **Line 21.**—"french maiquas, with whom was William Moody before mentioned, whom they endeavoured to save, but being driven down the River, he fell unhappily into another body of them, who most inhumanly tortured him, by fastning him to a stake, and roasting him alive; whose flesh they afterwards did eat; and being alarmd by a scowt of ours they endeavoured to way-lay them, being apprizd thereof and so far in the Enemys Country were forced to make a running fight with the loss of Lt. Wells." [MS.].

Page 49.

Line 12.—John Burt, not in manuscript. **Line 16.**—Ravill. [MS.]. **Line 20.**—Joseph Clesson and John Armes were taken from Deerfield, June 22, 1709, and the next day Jonathan Williams was killed and Matthew

NOTES. 17

Clesson mortally wounded. Lieut. Thomas Taylor and Issac Moulton, were also wounded but recovered. [N. H.].
Line 23.—Samuel Vetch is "Nicholson" in the manuscript.
Line 30-31.—Not in manuscript.

Page 50.
Line 15.—Preparing to govern the fleet. [MS.]. **Line 30** to **Line 29** of next page, found elsewhere with variations in the manuscript. **Line 31.**—The former name of Canada —see Gordon's *Geography*. [N. H.].

Page 51.
Line 12.—Oliver Cromwell. **Line 30.**—July the 15th. [MS.].

Page 52.
Line 2.—Massathusets. [MS.]. **Line 15.**—Leostaff. [MS.]. **Line 18.**—The Star, a bomb-ketch. Williamson. **Line 24.**—Col. Walton, "of new Hampshire". Taylor, Hobbey. [MS.]. **Line 25.**—Col. Joseph Whiting was from Connecticut. He graduated in Harvard College in 1690. Manuscript of W. Winthrop, Esq. [N. H.]. **Line 28.**—Toy. [MS.]. **Line 32.**—Redding. Williamson.

Page 53.
Line 34.—If the description of this bombardment read by our author, or described to him by one who was present —for undoubtedly, he was not there himself—truly suggested as he states, the lines that follow on page 54, the coincidence is remarkable. One would rather assume that he had been refreshing his memory of the events of Sir William Phips' career by reading a stray copy of Cotton Mather's *Magnalia Christi Americana* which he may have had in his library. In this now rare volume, he would have found, in the story of Phips' attack on Quebec, in 1690, the very same lines suggesting themselves to the learned Dr. Mather, and introduced with a similar phrase—"as the poet expresseth it." But we find the rhyme on p. 54 wanting in the manuscript, so the whole thing is undoubtedly one of Dr. Colman's intercalations—enforcing upon his author something closely akin to plagiarism.

Page 56.
Line 18.—Anselm de Castine ("Castine the younger"),

a son by an Abnaki woman, of Jean Vincent, Baron de Castine of Bigaduce. **Line 27.**—Winterharbour. [MS.].

Page 57.

Line 15.—"rapid and", not in manuscript. **Line 25.**—"rhine" for "bark". [MS.]. **Line 27.**—"Sixth of December where Mons. Vaudriel the Governr. and the Gent. there entertained him with great nobility." [MS.]. **Line 33.**—Trois Rivieres in Lower Canada. [N. H.].

Page 58.

Line 4.—Crossing the Lake, where they left them. [MS.]. **Line 6.**—Spring, while Our forces were engaging the Enemies abroad our frontiers were still infested at home. [MS.]. **Line 10.**—Col. Winthrop Hilton. **Line 16.**—June 23, 1710, says the monument over his grave. For a particular memoir of his life, the reader is referred to Farmer & Moore's *Collections*, I, pp. 241-251. [N. H.]. **Line 33.**—The same day that Colonel Hilton was killed, a company of Indians who had pretended friendship, who had been peaceably conversant with the inhabitants of Kingston, and seemed to be thirsting after the blood of the enemy, came into the town and ambushing the road, killed Samuel Winslow and Samuel Huntoon; they also took Philip Huntoon and Jacob Gilman, and carried them to Canada; where, after some time, they purchased their own redemption by building a saw-mill for the governor after the English mode. Belknap, I, 280. [N. H.].

Page 59.

Line 2.—Town of Exeter. [MS.]. **Line 15.**—These towns are in Connecticut. [N. H.]. **Line 19.**—Major Tyng was wounded by the Indians between Concord and Groton. He was carried to Concord and there died. Allen's *Hist. of Chelmsford*. [N. H.]. **Line 23.**—On the 20th of July, 1710, six men, Ebenezer Hayward, John White, Stephen and Benjamin Jennings, John Grosvenor and Joseph Kellogg, were making hay in the meadows, when the Indians who had been watching an opportunity to surprise them, sprang suddenly upon them, despatched five of them, and took the other, John White, prisoner. White spying a small company of our people at a distance, jumped from the Indian who held him, and ran to join his friends, but

NOTES.

the Indian fired after him and wounded him in the thigh, by which he fell; but soon recovering and running again, he was again fired at, and received his death wound. This was the last mischief done by the Indians at Brookfield. Whitney's *History of Worcester*. [N. H.]. **Line 29.**—They came to Saco. [MS.]. **Line 33.**—Jabez Garland. [MS.].

Page 60.

Line 4.—Where fowei [4] of the Enemy. [MS.]. **Line 11.**—Arruhawikwabenit. [MS.]. **Line 21.**—Several of them encampt. [MS.]. **Line 33.**—"Computed" replaces "not above". [MS.].

Page 61.

Line 19.—"April 23d", in manuscript. **Line 22.**—Thomas Downs and John Church. Belknap, I, p. 352. **Line 24.**—John Horn. [N. H.]. **Line 25.**—Humphrey Foss. [N. H.]. **Line 28.**—The N. H. reprint reads "Winnepiseogee".

Page 62.

Line 1.—"Col. Nicholson being not satisfyed with the Reduction of Anapolis alone, which was so prejudicial to our Trafick and Comerce, being a receptacle for all the Pyrates that came from Martincco or any other of the french Plantation, resolved againe to strike at Canada, as the spring and chiefe Magazine of all their territories; Upon which he went to England....." [MS.]. **Line 2.**—Not in manuscript. **Line 21.**—From this point to line 11 of the following page, the author has quoted almost literally from the *Boston News Letter*, No. 379. **Line 32.**—"12 men of war, 43 Transports". [MS.]. **Line 34.**—John Hill, Walker's *Journal*. "Jack Hill in charge of seventeen of Marlborough's regiments."—Elliott.

Page 63.

Line 14-15.—not in manuscript.

Page 64.

Line 8.—This table was copied from Walker's *Journal*, and from that, it may be corrected. The names of three ships incorrectly spelled here according to Walker's list are the Swiftsure, Kingston and Mountague. The flag-ship's captain was George Paddon. Others were John Mitchel,

NOTES.

Robert Arris, George Walton, Henry Gore, John Cockburn, Augustin Rouse, John Winder, Issac Cook. Officers previously mentioned (p. 62) were H. Disney, Richard Kane, P. Kirk, Jasper Clayton and William Windress. There were 440, not 444 men aboard the Swiftsure. **Line 28.**—"The first harbour...River, and ye same Night by a North East storm, severall transports with Eight hundred men were cast away, which put the whole fleet into a strange consternation; from thence they went back to Spanish River, wch. was sixty Leagues, where they held a council of war, whether to proceed or not, which was determined in ye Negative. It was then movd whether they should attack Placentia, but that would neither do, for some pretended they should want provisions. Whereas many among them well disposd to ye Crown and to the interest of New England, who were men of knowledge and integrity, and knew the whole state of Matters, were ready to assert the contrary, that they not only had provisions, but strength enough to proceed and that if they had taken the advice of our Pilots, this disaster would not have hapned." [MS.].

Page 65.

Line 12.—Cast ashore on Egg-Island. [MS.]. Little of this text is found in the original manuscript.

Page 66.

Line 10.—See Hovenden Walker's *Journal*.

Page 67.

Line 12.—"by order of Col. Vetch, with 60 men under his command," [MS.]. **Line 18.**—This to end of paragraph not in the manuscript.

Page 69.

Line 19.—"Seventy thousand Pounds." [MS.].

Page 70.

Line 4.—"King Henry the Seventh, which is Canada on the North and Nova Scotia on the South; In the year 1621 Sr Wm. Alexander had a Grant of it from King James, where he settled a Colony and possist it some years; after that Sr. David Kirk, who was proprietour as well as Governour; but did not Enjoy it long for to the surprise of all, it was afterwards given unto the French: However Oliver,

NOTES.

was Eagle-Eyd, and well knew the consequence that would redoun to the English, retooke it in ye year 1654; and altho upon the treaty with France he was earnestly solicited to surrender it would by no means consent, for that it was too great a jewel to bee parted with very soon. after the restoration it was again given up to the shame and scandal of ye Brittish Nation. The Unhappy disappointmt...." [MS.]. **Line 27.**—Plunder, and killed two Indians. [MS.].

Page 71.

Line 3.—Sinakes. [MS.]. **Line 5.**—Shacktains. [MS.]. The N. H. reprint modernizes these names. **Line 6.**—Gibbs. [MS.]. **Line 7.**—Anyone who has read the manuscript of Penhallow will exculpate the old-time compositor who failed on this name. It seems to be Brim or Brius. **Line 16.**—"Plantations" for "Wigwams." [MS.]. **Line 24.**—From Mr. Hilton's to Exeter, not in manuscript.

Page 72.

Line 3.—Cromwet. [MS.]. **Line 4.**—"100,000 ft. of Boards." [MS.]. **Line 5.**—Tole-end: in Dover. [N. H.] **Line 10.**—Nolton, in manuscript. **Line 27.**—Ebenezar Stephins. [MS.]. **Line 33.**—"August 24, being Lords day." [MS.].

Page 73.

Line 1.—"Next day a Scout was sent in pursuit, who found five oxen and ten horses, that were killd. Upon this it was believed their body was numerous, whereupon 100 men were raised, but missing their track, went beyond." [MS.]. **Line 3.**—Children belonging to John Waldron. See Belknap, I, 284. [N. H.]. **Line 7.**—Hester Jones. [MS.]. **Line 15.**—Davies. [MS.]. **Line 19.**—Stover, but being attacked by Lt. Heath, soon drew off. [MS.] Probably Storer. [N. H.]. **Line 27.**—Elisha Plaisted, from Portsmouth, and Hannah Wheelwright. **Line 32.**—Joshua Downing.

Page 74.

Lines 3 and 8.—Robison. [MS.]. Heard. See: Bourne, p. 278. **Line 11.**—Probably this amount is overstated. Elisha Plaisted's own letter asking to be redeemed says 50 Pounds were demanded. Bourne, p. 280. **Line 12.**—Johnson Harmon, later Colonel, of York, Me. He served under

NOTES.

Col. Shadrach Walton and Col. Thomas Westbrook. **Line 20.**—Samuel Moody, of Falmouth. **Line 30.**—This document was in the possession of Frederick Kidder, of Boston, in 1859, and was printed for the first time by him in that year. See: *The Abenaki Indians; their Treaties of 1713 & 1717*, etc. (Portland, 1859.) Many immaterial variations are found in Penhallow's text, though as one of the Counsellors of New Hampshire he was present. The signatures of the witnesses of this treaty are here reproduced from the above mentioned book.

Page 78.

Line 23.—Some inconsistencies in spelling; see p. 79, and reproduction of the manuscript of that page.

Page 80.

Line 4.—July 11, says Barstow, p. 123.

Page 81.

Line 26—This account, from line 30, p. 74, to this point, will be found in the *Provincial Papers of New Hampshire*, Vol. III, Part II, pp. 543-545.

Page 82.

Line 7.—Brunswick. [MS.]. This town was settled as early as 1675, by a Mr. Purchase, who lived near the head of Stevens' river and traded with the Indians, of whom he obtained grants of land; but the first settlements here were broken up in 1676. Sullivan, p. 177. [N. H.]. The N. H. reprint reads Brunswick, the original manuscript form. **Line 10.**—A Fishery at Small Point was also, etc. [MS.]. **Lines 12 to 18.**—Not in the manuscript.

Page 84.

Line 27.—John Penhallow, son of the author, born January 13, 1693, died before 1736, lived at Georgetown, Hanover Island or Arrowsick. See *Register*, XXXII, 21—28.

Page 85.

Line 1.—About the first of August, 1721. The Indians numbered 200. **Line 7.**—Probably Father De La Chasse, afterwards Superior General of the missions to New France. [N. H.]. **Line 9.**—Croisil, Croisel, Croissel, a French officer. Baron de St. Castine, a very extraordinary character. According to Voltaire, and the Abbe Raynal, he

NOTES.   23

had been Colonel of the regiment of Coriagon, in France. He was a man of family and fortune: he came to America in 1670, and settled among the Penobscot Indians, married a daughter of the Chief, and had several other wives. By the treaty of Breda, the territory beyond the Penobscot was ceded to France, and Castine lived within that country. Some difficulty arose about a cargo of wine, which was landed in the country, and a new line was run by the English, by which the place of landing, together with Castine's lands, was taken within the English Claim. Andross, in his expedition before named, plundered Castine's house of everything valuable, in his absence. This base act so exasperated him, that he used his exertions to inflame the Indians against the English, which he effectually did, and their chief supplies of arms and ammunition were furnished by him. He had an estate in France, to which he retired when the French lost their possessions in that part of the country. See Sullivan's *Hist. of Maine*, pp. 93, 158, 226. —Vol. I, *Hist. of N. Hampshire*, pp. 195, 196. [C.]. If we name this war from those that occasioned it, we may call it Castine's war; but the French, perhaps, would call it Andross' war. Drake's *French and Indian Wars*, p. 164. [C.]. **Line 17.**—Whose Captains were Moodey, Harmon, Penhallow, Barker, Richardson, Wainwright and Gookin. [MS.].

Page 86.

Line 1.—150 more. [MS.]. **Line 4.**—Jesuit. [MS.]. **Line 10.**—Williamson says "we lost five men." **Line 33.**—And it happening to be dark before they got up to Merry-meeting-bay, etc. [MS.].

Page 87.

Line 19.—About the year 1720, Capt. Thomas Baker of Northampton, in the county of Hampshire, in Massachusetts, sat off with a scouting party of thirty-four men, passed up Connecticut river, and crossed the height of land to Pemigewasset river. He there discovered a party of Indians, whose Sachem was called Walternummus, whom he attacked and destroyed. Baker and the Sachem levelled and discharged their guns at each other at the same instant. The ball from the Indian's gun grazed Baker's left eyebrow, but did him no injury. The ball from Baker's gun went through the breast of the Sachem. Immediately upon being wounded, he leaped four or five feet high, and then fell instantly dead. The Indians fled to the river; Baker and his party pursued, and destroyed every one of them. They had a wigwam on the bank of the river, which was nearly filled with beaver. Baker's party took as much of it as they could carry away, and burned the rest. Baker lost none of his men in this skirmish. It took place at the confluence of a small river with the Pemigewasset, between Plymouth and Campton, which has since had the name of Baker's river. Farmer's & Moore's *Collections*, III, p. 100. [N. H.].

Page 88.

Line 8.—"Firing", an obvious misprint, is "fixing" in the manuscript.

Page 92.

Line 10.—Manuscript reads "several others," for Sailors. Line 15.—"Seventy Men". [MS.]. Line 18.—Wenpague. [MS.]. Line 34.—Bradstreet. [MS.].

Page 94.

Line 7.—Bradstreet. [MS.]. Line 11.—Capt. Blyn came from Boston. [MS.]. Line 13.—"24 Captives; wch was a very happy juncture of coming at that time for that the Enemy had resolved in an hour after to put them all to Death". [MS.]. One example out of many instances in which the manuscript statement is longer and more detailed than that of book. Line 18.—Astagenesh. [MS.]. Line 26.—Scalp for every male Indian of the age of 12 years upwards. [MS.]. Line 31.—Thirty pounds, and all regular detached forces, fifteen pounds. [MS.].

Page 95.

Line 6.—Three were killed and three wounded. *N. E. Hist. Gen. Reg.*, XXXII,, p. 22. Line 24.—Shadrach Walton commanded the New Hampshire troops in the attack on Port Royal. He was one of the New Hampshire Council. Line 26.—Robert Temple, a former Irish army officer. Line 31.—Yet one of our captives have since reported that five of ym were slain in ye engagement. [MS.].

NOTES.

Page 96.

Line 4.—"After the Enemy had made this Descent, we were informed that in their coming they beseiged St. Georges some days, where they killed five men; and then dispersing into small parties, did much mischiefe; the last that fell this year was a Man at Ninchewanock while he was at work in his field." [MS.] **Line 19.**—the same time, "with 100 more". [MS.]. N. H. reprint reads Ameriscoggin. **Line 20.**—"save burning the Fort and some Empty Cottages." [MS.] **Line 21.**—Wigwams. Westbrook writes that "the Fort was 70 yards in Length and 50 in bredth, Well Stockado'd 14 foot high furnisht with 23 houses Built regular." *Westbrook Papers*, p. 15. **Line 24.**—Captn. Sayward also from York, with a Company of Volunteers went so far as the White Hills, one hund. miles into the Enemys Countrey, but mett with ye like misfortune for he could not discover ye track of one Indian; the report which same gave at their return, was, that Saco River had its spring from the foot of those hills; that it was so steep on the S. E. side that none could ascend ym, but seemed severall miles in height, and that the clouds broke upon it—a great way below the top: From ye clouds downwards the mountain was covered wth. snow but above was nothing but shining rocks, which glittered like the Sun in its meridian. Some of the old Indians, have reported that in ye night these rocks appear heighest, and the lustre so great as to Extend its influence a considerable way off; which have caused some to imagine that severall Carbuncles are lodged there. [MS.]. **Line 27.**—"At Roger Deering's Garrison house in June, took 3 of Larrabee's children." Willis, II, p. 34. **Line 28.**—Mrs. Dearing was the wife of Roger Dearing, who lived on a farm since well known by the name of Nonesuch. Hutchinson informs us that the Indians also took three of his children as they were picking berries, and killed two other persons. [N.H.]. **Line 29.**—Mary Scammond, John Hunnuel and a son of Robert Jordan. [MS.]. One of the soldiers was Sergeant Chubb. **Line 31.**—"Trustrum Herd". [MS.]. Tristram Heard, says Dr. Belknap. [N. H.]. **Line 34.**—"Rawlings". [MS.]. See a long note on the above attacks in Belknap, II, p. 54.

NOTES.

Page 97.

Line 2.—"They shot two". These persons were killed on the 14th of August. [N. H.]. **Line 3.**—Rev. Joseph Willard graduated at Yale College, 1714, and was settled at Sunderland, from whence he removed to Rutland, and on the 12th July, 1721, was invited to settle in the ministry. The day of his installation was deferred on account of the discouragements of the times, till the fall of 1723, when he was cut off by the enemy. The following account of his death, and other Indian depredations, is given by Mr. Whitney, in his History of Worcester county.

As Deacon Joseph Stevens and four of his sons were making hay in a meadow, at Rutland, on the 14th August, 1723, they were surprised by five Indians. The father escaped in the bushes; two of the sons were slain, and two, Phineas and Isaac, were made prisoners. Two of the five Indians waylaid a Mr. Davis and son, who that afternoon were making hay in a meadow not far off, but weary of waiting, they were returning to the others, and met Mr. Willard in their way, who was armed. One of the Indian's guns missed fire, the others did no execution. Mr. Willard returned the fire and wounded one of them, it is said mortally; the other closed in with Mr. Willard; but he would have been more than a match for him, had not the other three come to his assistance; and it was some considerable time before they killed Mr. Willard. Phineas Stevens, above mentioned, was the celebrated warrior in the Cape Breton war; and the one who so bravely defended Charlestown, N. H., on the 4th of April, 1747, when attacked by 400 French and Indians under Mons. Debeline. [N. H.]. **Line 23.**—"some did it because of the pleasancy of his conversation, others for fear of what might happen because of the Enemy who seemed to threaten". [MS.]. **Line 25.**—"Piscataqua", for "Portsmouth". [MS.].

Page 98.

Line 6.—"........of their several tribes. They were moreover assured ye like reward for scalps as the English had. After that, they prayed thee Delivery of some prisoners wee had that were of kin, to ym. which was granted, and in the close of the Conference, they promised to take up the hatchet

NOTES.

in favour of ye English, agst all such as should enter into hostility against ym. At the desire of some Gentn, the Delegates of these Nations were entertained with the sight of a gun made by the ingenious Mr. John Pimm of Boston which was discharged of Eleven Bullets successively in the space of about two Minutes, each of which went thro a double door at about 50 yrds. distance; It was loaded but once for the Eleven shot and fired in the view of Col Schuyler, and the said chiefs. [MS.]. **Line 32.**—In this year, [1723] 2 persons, by the names of Smith and Bailey, were killed at Cape Porpoise; the former, on Vaughn's Island; the latter at a place near where the old meeting-house stood, on the sea-shore. Sullivan, 230. [N. H.].

Page 99.

Line 1.—October 11th, says Hutchinson, see p. 275. [N. H.]. **Line 3.**—Lower-Fort [MS.]. **Line 6.**—*Desert* it should be: a very large island covering the area of about 180 square miles, and nearly, all the waters of the Bay of Fundy, or Frenchman's Bay. It was named Monts Deserts by Champlain, in honour, perhaps, of De Monts, with whom he had formerly sailed. It was once called Mt. Mainsell by the English, which, Mr. Savage (in *Winthrop*, I, 23) thinks was so called in honour of Sir Robert Mansell, named in the great Charter.—Drake's *French and Indian Wars*, p. 220. [C.]. **Line 26.**—March 23, 1724, one Smith, Sergeant of the fort at Cape Porpoise, was killed. [N. H.]. **Line 27.**—Nathan Knight reports, April 19, 1724, "Indians yestarda Kil'd mr Michell, of Spurwink". *Westbrook Papers* p. 52. **Line 30.**—They then, ie. April 25, 1724. About the same time Mitchell was killed, John Felt, William Wormwell and Ebenezer Lewis, were killed at a saw-mill on Kennebeck river. [N. H.]. **Line 31.**—"Kennebunk, killed one Felt and two more of Lynn, ("Wormwood and Lewis", Williamson.) loading the sloop". [MS.]. See Bourne, p. 318, for full and correct account of this attack.

Page 100.

Line 5.—River, and fired so smartly, that it put ym. into a great consideration; the others discharged for some time with much bravery; but the Enemy were so numerous, and having the advantage of the first shot slew all, to three, who made their Escape unto ye Fort. Sylvanus Nock of Oyster River, who was Elder of the Church and a very worthy man, was the next that fell. [MS.]. **Line 11.**—Josiah Winslow, who graduated at Harvard College in 1721. [N. H.]. **Line 32.**—James Nock, says Dr. Belknap. [N. H.].

Page 101.

Line 2.—Thompson was killed in May, 1724. He lived on the road which leads from Quampeagan to Wells, at Love's Brook. One Stone was mangled and scalped near where Thompson fell by the same party, but he survived it, and lived to be an old man. Governor Sullivan, who knew him, says, "his life was miserable; he wore a silver caul on his head, went on crutches, had the use of only one hand, and was subject to strong convulsion fits." Sullivan, p. 252. [N. H.]. **Line 7.**—Colcord. Ephriam Stevens (?). **Line 8.**—Ebenezer Stephins. **Line 11.**—The late Samuel Welch, who died at Bow, 5 April, 1823, at the age of 112, recollected this event, and related to the writer of this note some of the particulars of it, about a month before his death. He stated that Peter Colcord, Ebenezer Stevens and Benjamin Severance, and two or three children of Mr. Stevens were taken by the Indians; that Colcord made his escape, and that the children of Mr. Stevens were afterwards redeemed. He also recollected the family of Jabez Colman, who was killed in 1724, (mentioned by Penhallow under that year) and stated that Colman was shot with two balls, one passing through his neck, and the other through his hip. [N. H.]. **Line 17.**—June 2, 1724, at five o'clock in the morning at York's Garrison. **Line 19.**—"Will". [MS.]. **Line 21.**— The other was John Carr. Belknap, II, p. 56. **Line 23.**— To Londonderry. **Line 27.**—Of Oyster Bay. Frost, p. 181.

Page 102.

Line 3.—At Portsmouth. [MS.]. **Line 4.**—"which was the first scalp taken since the breaking out of this war; altho the country in so short a time had spent 70 thousand pounds, which is surprizing to think off, considering so inconsiderable a handfull." [MS.]. **Line 5.**—July 9, 1724. Green, p. 58. **Line 28.**—Solloman Jordan near ye Garrison of Lieut. Dominicus Jordan at Spurwink. *West-*

NOTES.

brook Papers, p. 63. **Line 33.**—..........."leaving 25 packs, 12 blankets, a gun, some knives, hatchets, behind, some smoaked beef behind them............and several wounded. Simon Armstrong who belonged to us [?] was also wounded and Robt. Brownstone [?]. [MS.]. Rev. Dr. Holmes informs us, that in the copy of Penhallow in possession of the Massachusetts Historical Society, there is an advertisement at the end, desiring the reader to correct a great omission in page 105 (of this edition) viz. "In the article relating to Lieut. Bean and Company at the bottom of the page, it should have been added, one of their principal Indians was killed, and his scalp brought to Boston, for which said Bean and company received an hundred pounds." [N. H.].

Page 103.

Line 7.—An island on the east side of Kennebeck river, and about 10 miles from the main: celebrated as the place where Capt. John Smith landed in 1614; here he built some houses, the remains of which were to be seen, when Judge Sullivan wrote his History of Maine. It is spelt Moheagan. —Drake's *French and Indian Wars*, p. 222. **Line 14.**— *Indians*, "with some French that were supposed to be on board". [MS.]. **Line 28.**—June 27, 1724, Ebenezer Sheldon, Thomas Cotton, and Jeremiah English (friend Indian) were killed at Deerfield. July 10, Lieut. Timothy Childs and Samuel Allen, were wounded in returning from their labor in the field. Appendix to Williams' Narrative. [N. H.]. **Line 34.**—Ipswitch "with 16 more in 2 small vessels". [MS.]. Sylvester Lakeman. [MS.|.

Page 104.

Line 8.—In this engagemt. the Doctr. was wounded, in two places and one of his Ribs broken; Mr. Cut was also shot thro ye body, two more were hurted but in some time after they all recovered. The Enemy att this time were mostly become Pyrates, and yet a sufficient number of Cut throats lay sulking round the fronttiers which kept the country in a constant alarm: [M.S.]. **Line 13.**—This was on the 3d of August, 1724, and was the last mischief done at Rutland. [N. H.]. **Line 17.**—The enemy, four in number, made a breach in the roof, and as one of them was attempting to enter, he received a shot in his belly

30   NOTES.

from a courageous woman, the only person in the house, but who had two muskets and two pistols charged, and was prepared for all four; but they thought fit to retreat, carrying off the dead or wounded man. This was on the 6th of August. [N. H.]. Line 22.—Jeremiah Moulton. *Westbrook Papers*, p. 56. Bourn, (for Brown). [MS.]. Jonathan Bean. *Westbrook Papers*, p. 54. Sec. Willard wrote an order to go to Narridgwalk—"you must be sure to take Lt. Bane with you as your Pilot, who knows all that countrey." He mentions Bourn and Jo Bean. For Bane see Bourne, p. 261. For Capt. Johnson Harmon, of York, see Baxter, p. 236. At Georgetown, November 25, 1720, Capt. Johnson Harmon was Commissioner and Joseph Bean sworn Interpreter. Baxter, p. 282. **Line 24.**— "After they landed, they mett in with Abomizeen, who had slayn an Englishman the day before at Richmond; whom they no sooner shot but he jumpt into the river, and drowned himself." Also, "Ticonic, at Richmond," for Triconnick. [MS.]. Our forces at their first entering into the whale boats, being afraid, they might bee discovered went down the river, untill twas dark; at wch. instant [?] it was reported that, five cannoos from Penobscot went up the River and saw them, who informed their friends, that all below was well and no sign of hazard, which made ym all secure. [MS.]. **Line 28**—they killd his Daughter, and tooke his Wife Captive, who gave 'em some discoverry of the state of the Enemy. Augst. 12, they (Capt. Harmon) gote within sight of the Fort, where were 60 fighting men and abt. 90 women and children; the enemy were so secure, that our men gote with in pistoll shot, before they were discovered; who then fired a full volley, but hurted none; upon which our Men fell on with great courage and resolution; The Enemy on this faced about and fired again, but afterwards fled with utmost precipitancy, some into their canoos, and others into the river, which was so rapid, that most of them were drowned; several gote over, which were pursued, and many of them killd after this our men returned to the Town, where they found Monsr Ralle, the Jesuit, who was a bloody incendiary, and instrumentall to most of the mischief that were done us, by animating the Indians, and insinuating

unto them how meritorious it was to destroy the English:
some say that quarter was offered him, which he refused, saying that he would neither give nor take any. Upon wch.
Lt. Jaques [?] broke open the door, and seeing him, loading
his gun, shot him thro ye head. A captive of ours, whose
name is Mitchell was inhumanely pierced by him with a
lancet during the Engagemt. but by care of the Surgeon,
afterwards recovered. Capt. Mog. who was one of their
chiefs, fired at severall, while in the house who wounded one
and killd another—upon which so exasperated our men, that
they broke upon the Door and shot him dead; his wife and
children were at same time slain with him. They then burnt
and destroyed their Corn with about 40 Cannoos: took three
bbs. of blankets, kettles, Beaver &c. As the night drew on,
they kept a strict watch surrounded the Indian houses,
wherein they lodgd; and in the morning found 26 of the
Enemies Dead bodies, wch. they scalpt, together with the
Jesuits; took alive 4 Indians, recovered three Captives, and
burnt all to ashes. This action was so great, considering
the difficulty of travelling thro so many swarms of flyes,
gnats and musquetoes at least 120 miles up the Enemies
Countrey; that it surmounted all other, ever since the
Narahgansett warr; [MS.]. **Line 32.**—According to later
authorities, they left Richmond, August 19th. **Line 34.**—
sixty Men, "and about 90 women and children". [MS.].

Page 105.

Line 25.—Sebastian Ralle died in the 67th year of his
age, after a painful mission of 37 years; 26 of which were
spent at Norridgwock. Previous to his residence at this
place, he spent six years in traveling among the Indian
nations in the interior parts of America; and in learning
most of their languages. "Il Scavoit presque toute les
langues, qu'on parle dans ce vaste continent." He was a
man of good sense, learning and address; and by a gentle,
condescending deportment, and a compliance with the
Indian mode of life, he obtained an entire ascendency over
the natives, and used his influence to promote the interests
of the French among them. "He even made the offices of
devotion serve as incentives to their ferocity; and kept a
flag, in which was depicted a cross, surrounded by bows and

NOTES.

arrows, which he used to hoist on a pole at the door of his church, when he gave them absolution, previously to their engaging in any warlike enterprise." A dictionary of the Norridgwock language, composed by Father Ralle, was found among his papers; and it is deposited in the Library of Harvard College. There is this memorandum on it: "1691. Il y a un an que je suis parmi les sauveges je commence a mettre en ordre en forme de dictionaire les mots que j'apprens." It is a quarto volume of about 500 pages. Belknap's *Hist. of N. Hampshire*, II, p. 60. Charlevoix *Nouv. France*, II, pp. 376-385. **Line 29.**—"by animating the Indians, and insinuating unto them, how meritorious it was to destroy the English".

Among other details of this victory is the following—"besides the fryer, who was so malignant against the English, that he was never more at ease, than when he was most Engaged in animating the Indians to blood and Cruelty." [MS.]. There is a valuable memoir of Ralle in the Collections of Massachusetts Historical Society, Vol. VIII, p. 250, in which his character is more favorably represented than in the above account: it seems that the account in the text is not perfectly correct. [N. H.].

Page 106.

Line 2.—Harmon swore in twenty-seven scalps at Boston, including Ralle's.—See *Mass. Archives*, 52:34. **Line 6.**—Penhallow, in the manuscript, marvels "nextly, that our forces should come so near, as to view their ground, and pastures, before they were discovered, and no sentinel out on Duty. And that so many of ym. should bee destroyed in so short a time with so little damage which by a modest computation, were upwards of eighty; besides the fryer." **Line 10.**—Hanscom. [MS.]. See White, p. 100. **Line 18.**—See Belknap, II, pp. 58-59. **Line 19.**—*September* 4, 1724.

The persons taken were Nathan Cross and Thomas Blanchard, who had been engaged in the manufacture of turpentine, on the north side of Nashua River, near where Nashua village now stands. At that time, there were no houses or settlements on that side of the river. These men had been in the habit of returning every night to lodge in a saw-mill on the other side. That night they came not as usual. An alarm was given; it was feared they had fallen into the hands of the Indians. A party consisting of ten of the principal inhabitants of the place started in search of them, under the direction of one French, a sergeant of militia. In this company was Farwell, who was afterwards lieutenant under Lovewell. When this party arrived at the spot where the men had been laboring, they found the hoops of the barrel cut, and the turpentine spread upon the ground. From certain marks upon the trees made with coal mixed with grease, they understood that the men were taken and carried off alive. In the course of the examination, Farwell perceived that the turpentine had not ceased spreading, and called the attention of his comrades to this circumstance. They concluded that the Indians had been gone but a short time, and must still be near, and decided upon an instant pursuit. Farwell advised them to take a circuitous rout, to avoid an ambush. But unfortunately he and French had a short time previous had a misunderstanding and were then at variance. French imputed this advice to cowardice, and called out, "I am going to take the direct path; if any of you are not afraid, let him follow me." French led the way and the whole party followed, Farwell falling in the rear. Their route was up the Merrimack, towards they bent their course to look for their horses upon the interval. At the brook near Lutwyche's (now Thornton's) ferry, they were way-laid. The Indians fired upon them, and killed the larger part instantly. A few fled, but were overtaken and destroyed. French was killed about a mile from the place of action, under an oak tree now standing in a field belonging to Mr. Lund in Merrimack. Farwell in the rear seeing those before him fall, sprung behind a tree, discharged his piece and ran. Two Indians pursued him: the chase was vigorously maintained for some time without gaining much advantage, till Farwell passing through a thicket, the Indians lost sight of him, and fearing he might have loaded again, they desisted. He was the only one of the company that escaped. A company from the neighborhood mustered upon the news of this disaster, proceeded to the fatal spot, took up the bodies of their friends and townsmen and interred them in the burying ground in Dunstable. Blanchard and Cross were carried to Canada: after remaining there some time, they succeeded by their own exertions in effecting their redemption and returned to their native town, where their descendants are still living.—*Relation of Col. E. Bancroft, of Tyngsborough, Mass.* [N. H.]. **Line 21.**— Thomas Lund, born September 9, 1682, was slain by Indians September 5, 1724, at Naticook, opposite Dunstable. **Line 30.**—September 7, 1724. And four children captured. Nathaniel Edwards not in the manuscript nor are the next 15 lines.

Page 107.

Line 12.—For "fresh" the manuscript reads "300". **Line 19.**—The two paragraphs ending this page are contracted from nearly two pages of the manuscript. This statement appears: "The last damage that happened this year was the killing of one Allein of Saco who had upwards of 20 Pounds in Province bills... with him (illeg.). Capt. John Lovewell lived in Dunstable, New Hampshire, then Massachusetts. "He was a son of Zacheus Lovewell, an ensign in the army of Oliver Cromwell, who came to this country and settled at Dunstable, where he died at the age of one hundred and twenty years; the oldest white man who ever died in the State of New-Hampshire."—*Farmer's & Moore's Collections*, III, p. 64. [C.]. Interesting but, excepting as to his residence, not true. He was born October 14, 1691, and was the son of John and Anna (Hassell) Lovewell, of Dunstable. His father died about 1755, aged about 95. His grandfather was John Lowell spelled also Lowel, Lowwell, Lovill or Lovwell,—a Boston tanner before 1665, who removed to Dunstable about 1683. Mr. Ezra S. Stearns, in his *Early Generations of the Founders of Old Dunstable*, (Boston, 1911), has with characteristic accuracy cleared up Lovewell's genealogy, for the first time.

Page 108.

Line 1.—"The Governments being apprehensive of the vile perfidy of the french at Canada in supplying the Indians with all Necessary stores of Warr, notwistanding the Peace at Ryswick". [MS.]. Montreal not mentioned in

NOTES. 35

manuscript. Col. Schuyler of Albany and some Mohawks gave protection on the return. **Line 4.**—"Ryswick" for Utrecht. [MS.]. **Line 5.**—Samuel Thaxter. **Line 7.**—Theodore Atkinson. Page 120 of the original manuscript is contracted in a general way into the balance of this paragraph. **Line 25.**—See *N. H. Hist. Coll.*, II, p. 242. Our author attended this conference.

Page 109.
Line 22.—Lake Champlain.

Page 110.
Line 14.—The N. H. reprint reads Winnepiscogee. **Line 21.**—The brave company, with the ten scalps stretched on hoops and poles, entered Dover in triumph, and proceeded thence to Boston, where they received the bounty of one hundred pounds for each, out of the public treasury. Belknap's *Hist. of N. Hampshire*, II, p. 63. [C.]. **Line 26.**—Blankets, "which is not usual". [MS.]. **Line 27.**—"severall". [MS.].

Page 111.
Line 2.—Maquoit is a bay, which lies about 20 miles north of Cape Elizabeth. Sullivan, p. 14. [N. H.]. **Line 13.**—"But when he got to the garrison abt. 12 of ym. went out ye next day unto the place where he had slain ym & skind another off his head that he might be entitled unto ye bounty which was accordingly done." [MS.]. **Line 23.**—"They then went to Scarborough where they killed many more beside horses and burnt some houses." [MS.]. **Line 27.**—"Mr. Tarbox's son at Winter Harbour was killed" [MS.].

Page 112.
Line 8.—Situated on the upper part of the river Saco, then 50 miles from any white settlement, (ib. 1, 27,) which had been the residence of a formidable tribe, and which they still occasionally inhabited. It is in the present town of Freyeburg, Maine. Belknap's *N. Hampshire*, p. 63. —Drake's *Appendix to Indian Wars*, p. 33. [C.]. **Line 9.**—About half way between a remarkable Indian mound in Ossipee, and the western shore of Ossipee Lake, "are the remains of the fort built by the brave Capt. Lovewell, just before he fell in the celebrated battle near Lovewell's

NOTES.

pond, in Freyeburg."—Farmer's & Moore's *Coll.*, I, p. 46. [C.]. **Line 17.**—Some call this Lovewell's pond; but Lovewell's pond is in Wakefield, where he some time before captured a company of Indians, who were on their way to attack some of the frontier towns.—Drake's *Appendix to Indian Wars*, p. 331. [C.]. **Line 34.**—Seth Wyman of Woburn. See Sewall, *Hist. of Woburn, Mass.*, (Boston. 1868.)

Page 113.

Line 1.—This Indian has been celebrated as a hero, and ranked with the Roman Curtius, who devoted himself to death to save his country. (See Hutchinson's *History*, II, p. 315.) Having been on the spot where this celebrated action happened, and having conversed with persons who were acquainted with the Indians of Pigwacket, before and after this battle, I am convinced that there is no foundation for the idea that he was placed there to decoy; and that he had no claim to the character of a hero. The point on which he stood is a noted fishing place; the gun which alarmed Lovewell's company, was fired at a flock of ducks; and when they met him, he was returning home with his game and two fowling pieces. The village was situated at the edge of the Saco river, which here forms a large bend. The remains of the stockades were found by the first settlers, forty years afterward. The pond is in the township of Frieburg.—Belknap's *Hist. of N. Hampshire*, pp. 65-66. [C.]. **Line 8.**—Both parties advanced with their guns presented, and when they came within "a few yardes," they fired on both sides. "The Indians fell in considerable numbers, but the English, most, if not all of them, escaped the first shot."—Drake's *Appendix to Indian Wars*, p. 332. [C.]. **Line 13.**—Hoping to be sheltered by a point of rocks which ran into the pond, and a few large pine trees standing on a sandy beach, in this forlorn place they took their station. On their right was the mouth of a brook, at that time unfordable; on their left, was the rocky point; their front was partly covered by a deep bog, and partly uncovered; and the pond was in their rear. The enemy galled them in front and flank, and had them so completely in their power, that had they made a prudent

NOTES. 37

use of their advantage, the whole company must either have been killed, or obliged to surrender at discretion. Belknap's *Hist. of N. Hampshire*, II, pp. 66-67. [C.]. **Line 28.**—Numbers are not given in the manuscript. Hutchinson and Symmes say 80; Belknap, 41, and Williamson, 63. **Line 34.**—There were ten men remaining at the fort to be saved by timely warning or to be secured for reinforcement. The strange penalty of namelessness was imposed upon this man by the Rev. Thomas Symmes in his Sermon —the first printed account of the engagement. Genealogical resiarch, nearly two centuries later, supplies the probable explanation of the reason why he was not publicly branded by name, the least that a deserter, if such he was, might expect. The facts are that he was a cousin of Lovewell— the son of Joseph who was a brother of Anna, Capt. John Lovewell's mother. His name was Benjamin Hassell. He was born August 9, 1701, at Dunstable. It seems that anonymity was the worst punishment that Symmes believed he could inflict upon so near a relative of the hero Lovewell without detracting from the glory of the family name. See Stearns, *Early Generations of the Founders of Old Dunstable*, Boston, 1911.

Page 114.

Line 13.—Josiah Farwell, Lovewell's brother-in-law, and Ensign Jonathan Robbins. Both of Dunstable.

The Indians invited them to surrender, by holding up ropes to them, and endeavoured to intimidate them by their hideous yells; till just before night, they quitted their advantageous ground, carrying off their killed and wounded, and leaving the dead bodies of Lovewell and his men unscalped.—Belknap's *Hist. of N. Hampshire*, II, p. 67. [C.]. **Line 21.**—"Wyman killd five or six Indians in the fight as ye lay behind a fallen tree. Davis had many a fair shott, and saw severall fall; he lost one joynt off of his thumb, had his gun broke in two," etc. [MS.]. **Line 22.**—Jonathan Frye, of Andover. **Line 23.**—Josiah Jones, of Concord. **Line 30.**—He fell about the middle of the afternoon. He was the only son of Capt. James Frye of Andover, graduated at Harvard College in 1723, and was chaplain of the company.—Drake's *Appendix to Indian Wars*, p. 334. [C.].

NOTES.

He was of Andover, and graduated at Harvard College in 1723. [N. H.]. **Line 31.**—Sergeant Jacob Fullam, of Weston.

Page 115.

Line 17.—This second edition was published about July 15, 1725. The title *Historical Memoirs* shows that our author did not see the now exceedingly rare first issue of Thomas Symmes' *Sermon* appearing about July 1st, entitled *Lovewell Lamented*, etc., long celebrated as the most valuable book of its size in the list of Americana. Rev. Thomas Symmes, of Bradford, Mass., whose Memoir of Lovewell's Fight is published entire in the first volume of Farmer & Moore's *Collections*. [N. H.]. **Line 25.**—Solomon Kies, of Billerica, Mass.

Page 116.

Line 4.—This paragraph is not in the manuscript. Unquestionably it is the intercalation of the Reverend Benjamin Colman. **Line 9.**—"So soon as the report came of Capt. Lovewell's disaster, fifty men from New Hampshire, well armed, and with twelve days' subsistence, marched thither to bury the dead and draw off the wounded, but were so miserably terrify'd that in a most shamefull and cowardly manner they returned without searching for the wounded or dead, or making the least discovery." [MS.]. **Line 10.**—This account of Lovewell's battle is collected from the authorities cited in the margin, and from the verbal information of aged and intelligent persons. The names of the dead, on the trees, and the holes where balls had entered and been cut out, were plainly visible, when I was on the spot in 1784. The trees had the appearance of being very old, and one of them was fallen.—Belknap's *Hist. of N. Hampshire*, II, p. 70. [C.]. **Line 13.**—"Col. Tyng from Dunstable with Capt. White now went to bury the dead, and make what discovery they could who ... [torn] where the fight was, buryed 12 of our men, and at a little distance found 3 Indians, lightly covded over whom they scalpt in expectation of some reward from the Government." [MS.]. **Line 16.**—Many of Lovewell's men knew Paugus personally. A huge bear's skin formed part of his dress. From Mr. Symmes' account, it appears that John

NOTES.   39

Chamberlain killed him. They had spoken together some time in the fight, and afterwards both happened to go to the pond to wash out their guns, which were rendered useless by so frequent firing. Here the challenge was given by Paugus, "It is you or I." As soon as the guns were prepared, they fired, and Paugus fell.—Drake's *Appendix to Indian Wars*, p. 234. [C.]. **Line 27.**—This paragraph not in the manuscript, but after a reference to 1st Samuel, 28:10, there follow some reflections on the notorious fact "that Evill spts. in ye Oracles of the Heathen have often foretold future contingencies; which is a mystery of providence in permitting ym to bee instruments of such revelations, and is very often for ye tryall of some, and the terrour of others. But the Devill by his wonderfull sagacity judgmt. and foresight, who is transendently superior unto any mortall might in an extraordinary manr. conjecture this, by the number of one and the other, together with the advantages that probably would happen, and by other symptoms beyond the reach of . . . . [illeg.] to penetrate into."

Page 117.

Line 3.—This was one of the most fierce and obstinate battles which had been fought with the Indians. Then had not only the advantage of numbers, but of placing themselves in ambush, and waiting with deliberation the moment of attack. These circumstances gave them a degree of ardor and impetuosity. Lovewell and his men, though disappointed of meeting the enemy in their front, expected and determined to fight. The fall of their commander and more than one quarter of their number, in the first onset, was greatly discouraging; but they knew the situation to which they were reduced, and their distance from the frontiers, cut off all hope of safety by flight. In these circumstances, prudence as well as valor, dictated a continuance of the engagement, and a refusal to surrender; until the enemy, awed by their brave resistance, and weakened by their own loss, yielded them the honor of the field. After this encounter, the Indians resided no more at Pigwacket, till the peace.—Belknap, II, p. 69, 70. [N. H.].

With all men of his time on the exposed frontiers of New England, Lovewell must have had an inborn hatred of the

40   NOTES.

Indian. As a youth he had lost many neighbors by the
Indians and within a period of a single month, he had lost
by the same enemy, a grandfather, a grandmother, an uncle
and two other relatives. But this expedition of his volun-
teer company to Pigwacket was undoubtedly undertaken
chiefly for profit, pure and simple. Several others were
out hunting for scalps for each of which the General Court
of Massachusetts had offered 100 Pounds currency. The
expedition was, in short, a prosaic "big game" hunting
trip, with the added zest of prospective commercial gain,
much as the modern sportsman seeks excitement and ivory
in Africa today. Insular tradition has praised these pot-
hunters into heroic proportions. The roll of the 47 men,
including officers, in this so-called Third company may be
found in the *N. E. Hist.-Genealogical Register*, July, 1909,
correctly given for the first time. **Line 9.**—Edward Lind-
field of Nutfield. **Line 18.**—"Upon" to the end of the
paragraph, not in manuscript. **Line 26.**—"Saccarexis".
[MS.]. **Line 27.**—"Prisoner, so long kept at the Castle."
[MS.].

Page 118.

Line 5.—Col. Walton lived at Somersworth. He was
dismissed from service, and was succeeded by Col. Thomas
Westbrook. [N. H.]. **Line 6.**—"Jno. Wainwright," |MS.].
Line 22.—Williamson, II, p. 144, says June 20.

Page 120.

Line 33.—Benjamin Evans. **Line 34.**—John Evans
was scalped and the third was William Evans. The original
manuscript in the Library of Congress ends with this page.

Page 121.

Line 2.—The Indians had come down to Cochecho, with
a design to take the family of Hanson again. When they
had come near the house, they observed some people at
work in a neighboring field, by which it was necessary for
them to pass, both in going and returning. This obliged them
to alter their purpose, and conceal themselves in a barn,
till they were ready to attack them. Two women passed
by the barn while they were in it, and had just reached the
garrison as the guns were fired. They shot Benjamin

NOTES. 41

Evans dead on the spot; wounded William Evans and cut his throat. John Evans received a slight wound in the breast, which bleeding plentifully, deceived them, and thinking him dead, they stripped and scalped him. He bore the painful operation without discovering any signs of life, though all the time in his perfect senses, and continued in the feigned appearance of death, till they had turned him over, and struck him several blows with their guns, and left him for dead. After they were gone off, he rose and walked, naked and bloody, towards the garrison; but on meeting his friends by the way, dropped, fainting on the ground, and being covered with a blanket, was conveyed to the house. He recovered and lived fifty years. A pursuit was made after the enemy, but they got off undiscovered carrying with them Benjamin Evans, Jr. a lad of 13, to Canada, whence he was afterwards redeemed.—Belknap, II, 80. [N. H.]. See Goodrich, p. 490. **Line 31.**—August 25, 1725, deacon Field, deacon Childs, and others, were going up to the Green river farms, and were ambushed by the Indians, but they discovered the Indians, and John Wells discharged his gun at an Indian, who fell; the Indians fired at them, and wounded deacon Samuel Field, the ball passing through the right hypocondria, cutting off three plaits of the mysenteria, which hung out of the wound, in length almost two inches, which was cut off even with the body, the bullet passing between the lowest and the next rib, cutting, at its going forth, the lowest rib; his hand being close to the body when the ball came forth, it entered at the root of the heel of the thumb, cutting the bone of the fore finger, and, resting between the fore and second finger, was cut out, and all the wounds were cured in less than five weeks, by doctor Thomas Hastings.—App. to Williams' *Narrative*, p. 112. [N. H.].

Page 127.

Line 1.—Saguaroom, or Loron, a Penobscut. *N. H. Hist. Coll.* II, p. 262. **Line 3.**—Williamson says this Indian lived at St. Johns. **Line 4.**—Maganumber in *N. H. Coll.*, II, p. 262. **Line 9.**—This was called Dummer's Treaty.

Page 129.

Line 16.—The fifth, says Willis, II, p. 36.

Page 130.
Line 22.—Williamson, II, p. 147, says that the treaty was ratified in the meeting house ("concluded with a public dinner"—Smith's *Journal,* p. 47.) August 6, signed. ... .by Wenemovit, the chief Sachem, and twenty-five others of his associates. See No. 432, *Catalogue of the late Mr. George Brinley,* (Hartford, 1878.)

Bibliography

ABBOTT, J. S. C. History of Maine from the Earliest Discovery of the Region * * * until the Present Time. Boston, 1875.

BARSTOW, GEORGE. A History of New Hampshire, from its Discovery, in 1614, to the Passage of the Toleration Act, in 1819. Boston and New York, 1853.

BAXTER, JAMES PHINNEY. The Pioneers of New France in New England. Albany, 1894.

BELKNAP, JEREMY. The History of New Hampshire 3 vols. Boston and Phila., 1784, 1791, 1792.

BOURNE, EDWARD E. History of Wells and Kennebunk * * * Portland, 1875.

CHARLEVOIX, REV. P. F. X. History and General Description of New France. 6 vols. New York, 1900.

CHURCH, THOMAS. The History of Philip's War [etc.] also of the French and Indian Wars at the Eastward by S. G. DRAKE. Boston, 1827.

COOLIDGE, A. J. and MANSFIELD, J. B. A History and Description of New England, General and Local. Boston, 1859.

DRAKE, SAMUEL G. A Particular History of the Five Years French and Indian War in New England and Parts Adjacent, etc. Boston, 1870.

FARMER, JOHN and MOORE, J. B. *Collections Topographical, Historical and Biographical*, relating principally to New Hampshire. 3 vols. Concord, 1822-1824.

FROST, JOHN. Indian Wars of the United States; from the Earliest Period to the Present Times * * * New York and Auburn, 1856.

GREEN, SAMUEL A. An Historical Sketch of Groton, Mass. 1655-1890. Groton, 1894.

HOLMES, ABIEL. The Annals of America, from the Discovery by Columbus in the year 1492, to the year 1826. 2 vols. Cambridge, 1829.

BIBLIOGRAPHY.

KIDDER, FREDERIC.   The Abnaki Indians, their Treaties of 1713 and 1717, and a Vocabulary.   Portland, 1859.

———Expeditions of Capt. John Lovewell and his Encounters with the Indians, including a particular Account of the Pequauket Battle, etc.   Boston, 1865.

SEWALL, SAMUEL.   History of Woburn, Middlesex Co., Mass. [1640-1860]   Boston, 1868.

SULLIVAN, JAMES.   History of the District of Maine, Boston, 1795.

WALKER, HOVENDEN.   A Journal or Full Account of the late Expedition to Canada, etc.   London 1820.

WESTBROOK, COL. THOMAS.   Letters of, and others relative to Indian Affairs in Maine.   W. B. Trask, editor.   Boston, 1901.

WHITE, REV. HENRY.   Indian Battles with Incidents in the Early History of New England.   New York, 1859.

WILLIAMSON, W. D.   The History of the State of Maine.   [1602-1820] 2 vols.   Hallowell, 1832.

WILLIS, WILLIAM.   Journals of the Rev. Thomas Smith and the Rev. Samuel Deane, etc.   Portland, 1849.

Index

Abbercromy, Abbercromby, Capt., 54, 55.
Accadia L', 18, 28, 70, 109.
Adams, Capt., at Port Royal, 55.
Adiawando, Pennecook Chief, 2.
Aeneas, Indian of St. John's, 78, 79.
Ahanquid, Chief, 120.
Albany, [N. Y.], 20, 58, 63.
Alexander, Sir William, 51.
Allein, Capt., taken prisoner, 54.
Allein, Lewis, spy, 19.
Allen, Capt., of Westfield, skirmish with Indians, 24.
Amarascoggin, Amanascoggin, Ameriscoggin river, 77, 96, 121.
Amasccnty, Amassaconty, Amasecontee, 2, 48, 74, 75.
Amesbury, Amsbury, Aimsbury, attacks on, 25, 35, 48, 72.
Anne, Queen, 3, 54, 56, 62, 63, 69. 75
Annapolis Royal, [Port Royal], 17, 18, 19, 30, 31, 33, 42, 43, 50, 51, 62, 67, 69, 86, 94, 103.
Appleton, Capt., sent to Canada, 29.
Appleton, John, of Massachussetts, 80.
Appleton, Lt. Col., attack on Nova Scotia, 42.
Appleton, Samuel, of Massachusetts, 80.
Arexis, Arexus, Indian Delegate, 122, 127.
Armstrong, Laurence, Lt. Gov. of Nova Scotia or Acadia, 126.
Arreruguntanocks, (Indians), 129.
Arruhawikwabemt, of Naridgwalk, Chief Sachem, 60.
Arowsick, Congress at, 83, 85; attack on, 95.
Arteil, Artell, Mons., attack on Deerfield, 12, 49.
Ashley, Noah of Westfield, kills an Indian, 107.
Assacombuit, Assacambuit, Indian Sachem, 6, 30, 40.
Astagenash, Indians captured at, 94.
Atkinson, Mr., [Theodore], of N. H., 108.
Austin, Capt., attacked by Indians, 45.
Austin, Matthew, 25.
Augusta, [Phipsburg], Dr. Noyes' Stone Garrison, 82.
Ayers, Corp., of Winter Harbor, taken prisoner, 61.

Baker, [Barker], Lt., killed, 18.
Ballantine, Col., at Port Royal, 54.
Barnwell, Col., attacks the Tuscarorahs, 71.
Bartlett, Capt., at Port Royal, 55.
Bean, Joseph, Capt., Interpreter, 102, 104, 118, 135.
Belcher, Andrew, of Mass., 80.
Bellamont, Earl of, [Gov. N. Y., Mass., and N. H.], 77.
Bene, Capt., see Bean.
Berwick, Barwick, [Newichewannockj. 10, 14, 46, 72, 96, 100, 104, 114.
Black Point, [Scarborough,] Me., 9, 41.
Blin, Capt., 86, 94.
Bobasser, Mons., commanding French and English, 8.
Bomaseen, Bomazeen, Capt., Kennebec Indian Chief, 4, 38, 78, 79, 104.
Bonaventure, Mons., hostage, 55.
Bonovist, attack on vessels at, 26, 31.
Boocore, Mons., 23, 30.
Boston, 17, 20, 57, 62, 63, 82, 86, 91, 94, 97, 98, 107, 119, 120, 126, 129, 132, 135.
Bradley, Joseph, of Haverhill, attack on garrison, 10.
Brandon, Arthur, his wife and children slain at York, 9.
Briton Island, 50.
Broadstreet, Mr., at Winpaque, 92, 94.
Bromswick, [Brunswick], 82, 104.
Brookfield, [Quabaug], 24, 48, 49, 59.
Brooking, Samuel, shot at Arowsick, 95.
Brown, Capt., [John], 10, 16, 104.
Brown, Major., 53.
Buckley, Capt., 24.
Burnum, Elizabeth, killed at Kingston, 101.
Burt, John, lost, and dies of hunger, 49.
Butterfield, Samuel, captured at Groton, 38.

Cabot, Cobbet, Sir Sebastian, 51, 70.
Canada, 8, 14, 15, 17, 29, 30, 33, 37, 38, 49, 59, 62, 67, 69, 70, 85, 95, 101, 108, 121.
Canada tribes, 129.
Canady, Mr., 99.
Canso, 92, 93, 94, 97, 111.
[Cape, The], 94.
Cape Sables, 28, 32, 73, 103, Indians, 95, 122.
Carboneer, 31.
Carolina, 71.
Carpenter, William, of Kittery, 44.
Carver, Capt., 73.

46 INDEX.

Casco, [Portland], 2, 5, 6, 10, 20, 44, 74, 80, 129, 131.
[Castin], see St. Casteen.
Cayonges, [Cayugas], of the Five Nations, 25.
[Champlain, Lake], 109.
Charlestown, 26, 33.
Chasse, Rev. Peter de la, Jesuit, 85.
Chelmsford, 36, 59.
Chesly, [Chesley], Capt., of Oyster River, 45.
Chesley, George, 101.
Chester, 101.
Chichsha Indians, [Chickasaw], 71.
Chignecto, see Sachienecto.
[Choctaws], 71.
Church, Edward, 16.
Church, John of Cochecho, 61.
Church, Major, 16.
Clayton, Col., 63.
Cochecha, Cochecho, [Dover], 14, 59, 61, 96, 120.
Cockram, of Macquoit, 111.
Coffin, Peter, of N. H., 80.
Cogshel, Mr., at Mr. Desart, 99.
Colcard, Peter, of Kingston,101.
Cole, Capt., 16.
Cole, Isaac, at Wells, 73.
Cole, Serg., 45.
Coleman, Jahez, of Kingston, 106.
Concord, 114.
Connecticut, 25, 33, 52, 123, River, 20, 102.
Constant, Capt., 16.
Consumption Bay, 31.
Cook, Capt., 16.
Corwin, Jonathan, 80.
Councellours of the Mass. and New Hamp., 80.
Cowassuck, 20, 23.
Crepoa, privateer, 31.
Croizen, Mons., 85.
Cromett, Jeremiah, of Oyster River, 72.
Cromwell, Oliver, takes Nova Scotia, 51.
Cuningham, Mr., killed at Exeter, 71.
Cutt, Mr., at Penobscot, 104.

Damaris Cove, 86, 121.
Daniel, Benjamin, "let me kill one", [at Saco], 46.
Davis, Capt., 9, 73.
Davis, Eleazer, of Concord, 114, 115.
Davis, Moses, and son, killed, 101.
Davison, Capt., 55.
Deerfield, 8, 11, 23, 48, 49, 102.
D'Gouten, Mons., hostage, 55.
Dering, Mrs., of Scarborough, 96.
D'Young, pilot, 17.
Disnee, Col., 62.
Dissenters, 68.
Dover, [see: Cochecho and Toie-End], 19, 25, 40, 44, 71, 72, 104, 106.

Downing, Mr., at Wells, 73.
Downs, Thomas, of Cocheco, 61.
Drew, John, of Portsmouth, 97.
Dudley, Col., of Mass., 108.
Dudley, [Joseph], Gov., 2, 75, 77, 79, 80.
Dummer, Fort, 121.
Dummer, Hon. Wm., Gov. of Mass. 67, 69, 96, 123, 128, 130, 131, 132, 134.
Dunstable, [Nashua], 34, 36, 106, 107, 116.
Durell, Capt., of Fort Dummer, 121.
Dutch (and Indian) trade, 25, 98.
Dwight, Capt., of Fort Dummer, 121.
Dyer, Capt., 16.

Eaton, Moses, of Salisbury, 87.
Edgar, Mr., 85.
Edwards, Nathaniel, 106.
Eliot, Capt., 92, 93, 94.
Elliot, Robert, 80.
English, Joseph, (Friend Indian), 36.
Evans family, of Cochecha, 121.
Exeter, 25, 36, 44, 45, 48, 58, 71.

Falmouth, in Casco Bay, [see: Piscataqua], 126, 128, 129, 131, 132.
Farewell, [Josiah], 114, 115.
Ferrel, Capt., 33.
Five (Six) Nations, 25, 71, 97.
Fletcher, Pendleton, 59.
Forbes, Forbis, Capt., 53, 67.
Fowl, Capt., 28.
Fox Islands, twenty killed by enemy at, [Penobscot Bay], 103.
France, 17, 110.
French, the, [allies of the Indians and enemies of New England], 4, 5, 8, 11, 12, 13, 15, 17, 18, 19, 23, 25, 26, 28, 30, 33, 37, 40, 41, 43, 47, 49, 54, 56, 59, 67, 68, 69, 73, 86, 108.
French Indians, 106, 125.
French, Lt., of Dunstable, 106.
French River, 48.
Fry, Chaplain, 114.
Fullam, Jacob, 114.

Galeucias, [Galusha], Daniel, 35.
Gardiner, Rev. Mr., 27.
Gardner, Capt., 47.
Garland, Jacob, of Cochecho, 59.
Gaspey, Cape, 64.
George I, 89, 123, 130, 131.
George Town, 82.
Gibs, Col., 71.
Giles, Lieut., 18.
Gill, Capt., of Charlestown, 26, 27.
Gilman, sons of Jeremiah, 48.
Gilman, Stephen, ambushed, later killed at Kingstown, 44, 72.
Goff, Lt. Col., 54, 85.
Gold, Capt., of Conn., 25.
Golden, Mons., 94.

INDEX. 47

Gordon, Capt., of the Lowstaff, 52.
Goreham, Col., 16.
Green Islands, 17, 100.
Groaton, Groton, 24, 36, 38, 44, 102.
Guorden, Mons., 17.

Hadley, 24, 59.
Hall, Edward, 37.
Ham, Joseph of Cochecha, 96.
Hambrough, 82.
Hamilton, Mr., 85.
Hampton Village, five slain Aug. 5, 1703, 8.
Handson, Mr., 85.
Handy, Maj., 55.
Hanson, John, of Dover, 106.
Harman, Harmon, Capt., [Johnson], 74, 84, 86, 87, 95, 96, 104, 105.
Harmon, Col., 121.
Harmon, Mr., 45.
Harredon, [John], Capt., 16.
Harris, Capt., 32.
Hartford County, 13.
Harvey, Serg., 100.
Hastings, Capt., 71.
Haverhill, 10, 16, 25, 47.
Hays, James, of Amesbury, 48.
Head, [Heard], Tristram, 96.
Hegen, Indian Chief, 2.
Henry VII, 51, 70.
Herd, Lieut., son of, 72, 73, 74.
Higginson, John, 80.
Hill, Brigadier, 62.
Hill, Capt., of Wells, 29.
Hill, David, of Saco, 101.
Hilton, Col., 28, 40, 41, 42, 48, 58, 116; Maj., 10; Mr., 71; Capt., at Exeter, 36.
Hinsdel, Mehamen, 48.
Hobby, Sir Charles, 52, 53, 55.
Hoddy, Mr., of Piscataqua, 19.
Hoel, Mrs., of Spruce Creek, 31.
Hopehood, Indian Sagamore from Naridgwalk, 2.
How, Capt., 24.
Hudson Bay Co., 68.
Hunking, Mark, 80.
Hunnuell, Capt., 9.
Hunuel, John, of Scarborough, 96.
Hunuel, Stephen, 121.
Hussey, Widow[see Mussey].
Hutchins, David, of Kittery, 48.
Hutchins, Enoch, of Spruce Creek, 31.
Hutchinson, Col., 43.

Ipswich, 103.
Iroquois, Iroquoise, 25, 71, 97.
Iteansis, Penobscot Indian, 78, 79.

Jackoid, Penobscot Indian, 78, 19.
Jackson, Dr., of Kittery, 103, 104.
Jephson, Lt., 93.
Jerseys, the, 62, 63.
Jesuits, ["Fryars"], allies of the Indians, 4, 14, 23, 29, 37, 70, 82, 84, 85, 86, 94, 99, 105, 108.

Johnson, Lt., 54.
Jones, Easter, [Esther?], of Dover, 73.
Jones, Josiah, 114.
Jordan family, the, of Spurwink, 6.
Jordan, Robert, of Scarborough, 96.
Jordan, Solomon, of Spurwink, 102.
Joseph, St. John's Indian, 78, 79.

Kaine, Col., 63.
Kenebeck, Kennebeck, 74, 77, 78, 81, 82, 83, 85, 86, 91, 121.
Kenebunk, [Wells], 99.
Kent, Mr., of Casco, 7.
Kies, Solomon, 115.
Kingstown, [Kingston, N. H.], 36, 44, 45, 72, 101, 106.
Kirk, Col., 62.
Kirk, Sir David, 51.
Kittery, (Spruce Creek), 31, 33, 44, 48, 103.
Kizebenuit, Penobscot Indian, 78, 79.

Laborador, Terra de, 70.
Lafebure, Mons., French prisoner, 17.
Lakeman, Sylvanus, of Ipswich, drives off Indians, 103.
Lamb, Capt., of expedition against Nova Scotia, 16.
La'Motte, Fort, 48.
Lamper-Ele river, Lampreel, [Lamprey], attacks at, 14, 96.
Lancaster, attacked, 24, 27.
Lane, Capt., fight at Wells, 74.
Laribie, Thomas, of Scarborough, killed, 96.
Larraby, Capt., [Thomas], expedition against the French in Accadia, 28.
L'Have, Accadia, prisonerstaken at, 28.
Lett, Island of, 56.
Leverett, Mr., of Mass., Comm. to Five Nations, etc., 25, 43.
Levingston, Maj., expedition against Canada, 53, 56.
Levinston, Capt., of Conn., Comm. to Five Nations, etc., 25, 29.
Lingfield, Edward, of Lovewell's Company, 117.
Littlefield, Lt., [Josiah], of Wells, captured, 47; killed, 71.
Littlefield, Mrs., killed at York, 44.
Lotham, Capt., at St. John's, 30.
Loran, Capt., Chief, goes to Boston, 120; delegate, 130, 132.
Love, Mr., of Merrymeeting Bay, sent prisoner to Canada, 85.
Lovewell, Capt., of Dunstable, engagements with Indians, 107, 110, 112, 113, 114, 116.
Lynde, Benj., Mass., Councellor, 80.
Lyn, 99.
Lyon, Capt., at Port Royal, 55.

INDEX.

Macquas, [Mohawks], of the Five Nations, 25.
Macquoit, [Bay], soldier captured at, 111.
Magoon, John, killed, 59.
Mallegash, 93.
Maneval, Mons., Gov. of Nova Scotia, 51.
Marblehead, 32.
March, Col., attack on Pigwackett, 9, on Nova Scotia, 41.
March, Lieut., attacks Indians at Cape Neddick, 32.
March, Maj., [John], assaulted at Casco, 6.
Marlborough, attack at, 44, 59.
Martyn, Com., 52.
Mascareen, Capt., expedition against Canada, 53, 55, 126, 131.
Mason, Maj., at Berwick, 14.
Massachusetts, "the," 52, 75, 76, 83, 88, 90, 96, 108, 118; Bay, 122, 123, 124.
Mather Cotton, Rev. Dr., iii.
Matthews, Capt., hostage at Port Royal, 55.
Mauxis, Sagamore, 2, 6, 60, 81.
Mayhew, Thomas, vi.
Meador, Nathaniel, shot near Berwick, 14.
Meganumba, Indian Captain, 122, 127.
Menis, 17, 43.
Merrimack River, 72, 75, 77.
Merrymeeting Bay, attack on, 85.
Mesambomett, Amasconty Indian, 2.
Messisippi, [Mississippi], 68.
Mitchel, William, of Scarborough, shot, 99.
Mohawks, French, 36, 38, 45, 48, 106.
Mohegan Indians, 14, 20, 97.
Monhegen, 103.
Montreal Scout, robs an express, 28.
Moody, (Moodey), Capt., [Samuel], 30, 74, 84.
Moody, Wm., burned at the stake and eaten, 48, 49.
Moulton, Capt., [Jeremiah], at Naridgwalk, 99, 104, 105.
Mount Desart, 17, 99.
Mount-Real, [Montreal], 50, 66, 70, 108, 109, 110; river, 38.
Mullins, Maj., of Nova Scotia expedition, 53.
Mussey, [Hussey], Widow, a Quaker of Hampton, killed, 8.
Myals, Samuel, of Exeter, escapes, 37.
Myrick, Capt., 16.

Nalton, Serg., slain at Cape Neddick, 72.
Nantaskett, 16, fleets at, 42, 52, 64.
Narahamegock, Indians of, 75.
Naridgwalk, Naridwalk, Narridgwalk. [Norridgwalk], iv, 2, 28, 60, 74, 75, 99, 104, 107, 121, 122, 124, 128, 129, 132.
Nashaway, attack on, 24.
Nashua, see: Dunstable.
Natick Indians, (friend), 48.
Nawagen, Cape, [Boothbay, Lincoln Co., Me.], 119.
Neal Andrew, his garrison attacked, 10.
Nebine, Indian prisoner paroled, 117.
Neddick, Neddock, Cape, [York, Me.], attacks on, 32, 71, 72.
Newchawanick, Newichawannock, [later, Berwick], attack on, 72.
Newfoundland, attacks on, 26, 30, 68, 70.
Newhampshire. Newhamshire, 52, 75, 76, 80, 83, 88, 91, 101, 103, 108, 116. 118, 122, 126.
New London, Congress of Governors, at, 62.
Newton, Mr., taken at Passamaquady, 86.
New York, in attack on Canada, 50, 62, 63.
Nicholson, Sir Francis, 49, 50, 51, 52, 55, 62, 63, 66. 69.
Nock, Sylvanus, Elder, of Oyster River, slain, 100.
Noddles Island, [East Boston], encampment on, 63.
Northfield, attacks on, 97, 99.
North Hampton, Northampton, 15, 20, 22, 23, 48. 106.
North Yarmouth, garrison attacked, 121.
Norway, 82.
Nova Scotia, 18, 41, 50, 91. 122, 131.
Noyes, Dr., [Oliver], establishes a fishery, 82.
Noyes, Thomas, a Councellor of the Massachusetts, 80.

Oneydes, of the Five Nations, 25.
Onnondages, of the Five Nations, 25.
Ossipe, Ossipy, 61, 112.
Oxford, attack at, 104.
Oyster River, [Durham, N. H.], 19 25, 32, 44, 45, 47, 72, 100, 104.

Padishals Island, conference at, 85.
Paine Capt., captures French privateer, 33.
Palatines, murdered by Indians, 70.
Paris, Assacambuit visits, 40.
Parsons, Hannah, of Wells, 38.
Parson, widow and daughter, captive from York, 9.
Pascomuck, attack at, 15, 16.
Passamaquady, 17, 86.
Pastor, Paston, Capt., 52, 64.
Patrick, Col., 28.

INDEX.   49

Paugus, an Indian, 116.
Pearl, Wm., of Dover, slain, 40.
Pemaquid, 129.
Penhallow, Capt., conference with Ralle and others, 85; his garrison beset, 101; mentioned, 84, 95.
Penhallow, Samuel, Councellor for N. H., (a) 80.
Pennecook, [Penacook, Indian Settlement], 2, 75.
Penobscot, 2, 17, 56, 60, 70, 85, 86, 96, 104, 107; Bay, 118, 121; Tribes, 120, 122, 124, 125.
Pensilvania, 63.
Pequod Indians, [friend], 14.
Perpooduck, [Falmouth], 6, 101.
Philadelphia, 62.
Philipps Governor, 92.
Phillip, King, 40, 106.
Phippeny, Mr. of Casco, killed, 7.
Phips, Spencer, 79.
Phips, Sir William, Gov. of Mass., 51, 69, 77.
Pickernell, John, of Spruce Creek, shot, 72.
Pigeon, Capt., murdered, 67.
Pigwacket, Pigwackett, [Pequawkets] (Indians), 2, 8, 9, 48, 75, 112, 116.
Pim, Mr., of Boston, his repeating gun, 98.
Piscataqua, [Falmouth], 16, 19, 31.
Placentia, 26, 30, 33, 73.
Plaisted, Ichabod, Councellor, 80.
Plaisted, John, Councellor, 80.
Plaisted-Wheelwright marriage at Wells, 73.
Plutarch, quoted, 41.
Plymouth, 100; Plimouth, 13, 16.
Ponds, the, 9.
Porposs, Porpas, Porpos, [Porpoise], Cape, 5, 81, 111.
Port Rosua, [Port Roseway], prisoners taken, 28.
Port Royal, see: Annapolis Royal.
Portsmouth, 8, 41, 74, 80, 91, 97, 114.
Prebfole, Benjamin, of York, killed, 58.
Prescot, Capt., chases Indians, 24.
Price, Capt., at Haverhill, disperses Indians, 47.
Privateers, French, on New England coast, 31, 33.

Quabaug, [Brookfield], engagement near, 24.
Quakers, 8, 63, 106.
Quebeck, 47, 57, 65, 66, 70, 99, 108, 109, 110.
Quinsey, Edmund, Commissioner, 79.

Ralle, (Rallee), [Rasles], Sebastian, Jesuit missionary, 85, 105, 108.
Ravell, Mons., attacks Deerfield, 49.

Rawlins, Aaron, of Lamper-Ele River, killed, 96.
Reading, attack on, 36.
Reading, Col., attack on Port Royal, 52, 53, 55.
Rednap, Col., attack on Port Royal, 53.
Reed, Robert, of Kittery, killed, 48.
Rhode Island, 33, 52, 123.
Richmond, attack on, 96.
Richmond's Island, a sloop recaptured, 32.
Riddle, Capt., of the Falmouth, 52.
Ring, Joseph, burned at the stake, 10.
Robbins, Mr., of Lovewell company, wounded, 114.
Robinson, Capt., at Wells, killed, 74.
Robinson, Capt., in naval engagement, 92, 93.
Rochfort, Capt., of the Star Bomb, 52.
Rockamagug, soldiers at, 121.
Rogers, Capt., expedition against Canada, 16.
Rogers, John, of Kittery, wounded, 31.
Rolph, Rev. Mr., of Haverhill, slain, 47.
Rouse, Capt., of the Charlestown, 33.
Royal, Michael, of Marblehead, cut in pieces at Cape Sables, 32.
Rutland, Rev. Mr. Willard slain, 97; attack on, 104.
Sachenecto, [Chignecto], French and Indians from, 43.
Saco, attack on, 6, 101.
Saco Pond, Lovewell's fight begins, 112.
Saco River, Indians killed and captured on, 60; Indians of, 74, 77.
St. Casteen, [Castin], of Penobscot, 17, 56, 57, 85.
St Georges, 85, 91, 99, 100, 103, 118.
St. John's burned, 27; attack on, 30; Indian delegates from, 74, 78.
St. John's River, Indians of, 75, 77.
St. Laurence Bay, 50.
St. Laurence River, (St. Lawrence's) 64, 70, 109; Gulph, 94.
Sampson, Indian commander attacks York, 9; assaults captives, 38.
Samuel, Capt., Indian, 4; attacks fishing vessel, 86.
Saquarexis, Indian hostage, 117.
Sauguaaram, alias Sorun [Loron], Indian Captain, 122.
Saunders, Capt., at Penobscot Bay, 118.
Savage, Capt., captured at Passamaquady, 86.
Sayward, Capt., expedition to the White Hills, 96.

Scales, William and Mathew, slain at Yarmouth, 111.
Scamond, Mary, of Scarborough, captured, 96.
Scarborough, attacked, 6, 96.
Scatacook Indians, entertained in Boston, 97.
Schuyler, Col., warns Deerfield, 11; and Dunstable, 34.
Segmore, Col., expedition against Canada, 62.
Senakees, Senneches, of the Five Nations, 25, 71.
Severns, Ephraim, of Kingston, taken to Canada, 101.
Shacktaus, [Choctaws], attack Carolina, 71.
Shamblee, 57; fortification at, 109.
Shapleigh, Mr., killed at Kittery, 32.
Sharkee, Mons., 17.
Sheldon, Mr., brings forty-five captives from Canada, 37.
Shute, Samuel. Capt. Gen., Mass. Bay, etc., 83, 85, 91.
Simmo, Capt., Indian orator, 3.
Simsbury, attack on, 59.
Smith, Capt., of Port Royal expedition, 16.
Smith, Thomas, of Chester, captured and escaped, 101.
Soaper, Alexander, knocked on the head, 121.
Southack, Capt., 8, 16, 52, 53, 94.
Spanish River, 65, 77.
Spencer, John, killed, 73.
Spencer, Major, ("Blew" regiment), Nova Scotia expedition, 42.
Springfield, remarkable acuity of hearing of citizens, 16.
Spruce Creek, attacks on, 31, 71, 72.
Spurwink, twenty-two of the Jordan family killed and taken, 6; twenty-one years later, Solomon Jordan killed, 102.
Stebbins, Benoni, of Deerfiel, repulses Indians, 12.
Stephens, Capt., fails as scalphunter, 10.
Stephens, Ebenezer, of Kingstown, wounded, 72.
Stephens, Mr., two children captured, 101.
Stephins, Samuel, captured, 48.
Stoddard, Col., Commissioner for Mass., 118.
Stoddard, Rev. Mr., his account of the Deerfield massacre, 11.
Stover, [Storer?], Dependance. wounded, 73.
Stovers, Mr., of Cape Neddick, children killed and captured, 32.
Stratton, Mr., killed near Arowsick, 95.
Strong, John, wounded, 48.
Submission of Eastern Indians, 122.

Sudbury, Capt., recaptures plunder, 8, 44.
Supercass, Mons., [Subercase, Daniel d' Au.], attacks Newfoundland, 30; defends Port Royal, 42; surrenders Port Royal, 54, 55.
Symmes, Rev. Mr. Thomas, 115.

Tailer, Col., 52, 54.
Tailor, Edward, killed near Lampreel River, son and wife captive, 14.
Tailor, Maj., pursues Indians near Hadley, 24.
Tasket, Wm., of Oyster River, wounded, 19.
Taye, Capt., lost at sea with twenty-five men, 52.
Taylor, Rebekah, an incident of her captivity, 38.
Temple, Capt., engaged with superior force at Arowsick, 95.
Thaxter, Col., [Samuel], reinforces garrisons, 85; commissioner to Canada, 108.
Thomson, Miles, of Berwick, killed, son captive, 100.
Tibbits, Nathanael, of Dover, captured, 40.
Tilton, Lt., sorely beaten near Damaris Cove, 86.
Ting, Capt., receives bounty for scalps, 10; attacks Indians, 24.
Toby, James, shot near Kittery, 31.
Tole-End, [Dover], attacked, 72.
Tom, Capt., attacks Hampton Village, 8.
Townsend, Col., Commissioner to Five Nations, 25; in Nova Scotia expedition, 43.
Topsham, settlement began, 82.
Trescott, Lt., waylaid and wounded 111.
Trescot, Mr., captured in Merrymeeting Bay, 85.
Triconnick, [Winslow, Me.], 104.
Trinity, English settlements in, destroyed, 31.
Troy River, [Trois Rivieres], hospital at, 57.
Turner, Maj., assists in defence of Haverhill, 47.
Tuskarorahs, Col. Barnwell entirely routs them, 71.
Tuttle, Ensign, of Tole-End, slain, 72.
Tyng, Col., of Dunstable, buries Lovewell's dead, 116.
Tyng, Maj., of Chelmsford, killed, 59.

Utrecht, treaty of, violations of, by the French in Canada, 108.

Vaudriell, Mons., [Vaudreuil, Chevalier de, governor of Canada], arranges exchange of prisoners, 29.

INDEX. 51

Vaughan, Wil., Councellor of N. H., 80.
Vetch, Col., proposes reduction of Canada, 49, 50; Adjutant Gen., 52; at Port Royal, 53, 54, 55; to Canada, 63.
Virgin-Mountains, 64.
Virginia, Palatines in, murdered by Indians, 70.

Wadacanaquin, Indian delegate, 78, 79.
Wadley, Capt., ordered to Wells with Dragoons, 8.
Wainright, Capt., slain at Haverhill, 47.
Wainright, Capt., 84.
Wainright, Col., in Nova Scotia expedition, 42.
Waldron, Mr., of Cochecho, escapes 14.
Waldron, Richard, Councellor of N. H., 80.
Walker, Mr., chased by French privateer, 33.
Walker, Sir Hovendon, Admiral, expedition against Canada, 62.
Walton, Col., [Shadrach], of N. H., 52, 53, 60, 61, 63, 70, 84, 95, 118; witness of treaty 1713, 79.
Wanadugununbuent, Chief, of Penobscot, 2.
Wanton, Lt. Col., of "Blew" regiment, Nova Scotia expedition, 42.
Wanton, Maj., captures French privateer, 33.
Wanungonet, an Indian Sachem, 6.
Wanungunt, Chief of Penobscot, 2.
Warrueensit, Warraeensitt, delegate for St. John's, 78, 79.
Watanummon, Pigwacket Sachem, his intended treachery, 4.
Water-bury, three killed at, 59.
Wattanamunton, Chief from Pennacook, 2.
Weare, Nathan, Councellor for N. H., 80.
Webber, Samuel, shot, 71.
Weber, Michael, his wife inhumanly butchered, 6.
Watkins, Capt., killed, 97.
Wedgwood, John, of Exeter, carried to Canada, 59.
Welch, Capt., assists in destruction of Schactaus, 71.
Wells, 5, 8, 15, 29, 38, 44, 47, 49, 61, 71, 72, 73.
Wells, Capt., at Black Point, 9.

Wells, Capt., Thomas, of Deerfield, his garrison not attacked, 12; engagement with Indians on Conn. river, 102.
Wells, Lt., John, killed at French River, 48.
Wentworth, John, Councellor for N. H., 80.
Westbrook, Col., Chief in the eastern affairs, 96; at St. Georges, garrison, 99.
Westfield, 16; Capt. Allen rescues a captive, 24, engagement with Indians at, 106.
Wexar, Chief, from Amasconty, 2.
Wheeler, John, killed at Oyster River, 32.
Wheelwright, Capt., of Wells, 73.
Wheelwright, John, Councellor for Mass., 80.
White, Capt., buries the dead of Lovewell's company, 116; dies, 117.
White Hills, 96.
Whiting, Col., Joseph, commissioned from the Queen, (Canadian invasion), 52, 53.
Whiting, Maj., pursues Indians, 15; goes to meet invaders, 23.
Willard, Capt., puts enemy to flight, 24,; relieves a scout, 72.
Willard, Capt,, of sloop, at Blackpoint, 9.
Willard, Josiah, witness, 79, Secretary, 91.
Willard, Rev. Mr., of Rutland, killed, 97.
William and Mary, 51.
Williams, Rev. Mr., of Deerfield, captured, 12.
Williamson, Capt., in expedition against French, 16.
Windress, Col., of expedition against Canada, 63.
Winn, Joseph, escapes capture, 47.
Winnennimmit, Sagamore, 118.
Winnepisseocay, Winnepissocay Ponds, Col. Walton visits, 61; Capt. Lovewell at, 110.
Winniganse, captives taken at, 121.
Winslow, Capt., killed, 99, 100.
Winslow, Gov., 100.
Winter Harbour, [Biddeford], 5, 45, 56, 59, 61.
Wyat, Capt., in command of fort at Black-point, 9.
Wyman, Ensign, takes command of Lovewell's company, 114, 115; gets Captain's commission, 117.